Exploration in the World of the Ancients

DISCOVERY & EXPLORATION

Exploration in the World of the Ancients

JOHN S. BOWMAN

JOHN S. BOWMAN and MAURICE ISSERMAN
General Editors

Facts On File, Inc.

Exploration in the World of the Ancients

Facts On File, Inc.
132 West 31st Street
New York NY 10001

Library of Congress Cataloging-in-Publication Data

Bowman, John Stewart, 1931–
    Exploration in the world of the ancients / John S. Bowman ; Maurice Isserman and John S. Bowman, general editors.
        p. cm. —(Discovery and exploration)
        Summary: Discusses the voyages, navigation routes, and watercraft of explorers in the ancient world, from prehistoric times to the beginning of the Middle Ages.
    Includes bibliographical references (p.).
    ISBN 0-8160-5257-3
        1. Geography, Ancient—Juvenile literature. 2. Discoveries in geography—Juvenile literature. [1. Geography, Ancient. 2. Discoveries in geography. 3. Explorers.] I. Isserman, Maurice. II. Title. III. Series.
    G86.B68 2004
    910'.9'01—dc22   2003023033

Text design by Erika K. Arroyo
Cover design by Kelly Parr
Maps by Patricia Meschino and Dale Williams

Printed in the United States of America

VB FOF 10 9 8 7 6 5 4 3 2 1

This book is printed on acid-free paper.

To Francesca
who has supported my explorations all these years

NOTE ON PHOTOS

Many of the illustrations and photographs used in this book are old, historical images. The quality of the prints is not always up to current standards, as in some cases the originals are from old or poor quality negatives or are damaged. The content of the illustrations, however, made their inclusion important despite problems in reproduction.

Contents

PREFACE

Upon hearing that there is to be a book about discovery and exploration in the ancient world, many people express some surprise: "Were there explorers in the ancient world?" "What did they discover?" Such doubts are understandable because there are so many preconceptions and misconceptions about the nature of discovery and exploration. Although no single book can set the record straight for everyone, this volume—one in a set that will describe the entire history of the discovery and exploration of the world—should go a long way toward throwing light on this remote phase of history.

Perhaps the problem starts with the fact that, to put it politely, many people are a bit "shaky" when it comes to ancient history, so it is best to start by defining what is meant by the ancient world. Usually this is considered to begin with the first writing systems—which would be about 3500 or 3000 B.C. The time before that is then termed prehistory, a concept that recognizes the written record as the beginning of "history" as a discipline. To better understand how the world was actually opened up by and to human beings, however, this book does go back before the written record and recognizes that the first discoverers and explorers were, in fact, the nameless people who first moved into so many distant corners of the earth. Other histories of exploration tend to overlook these people. This book takes considerable pride in giving them their due.

Then, by longstanding agreement among historians in the Western world at least, the "ancient" period is considered to have ended about A.D. 500. Various events are traditionally singled out, but one in particular is regarded as the turning point: The last Roman emperor in the West was deposed in 476 by a Germanic leader, Odoacer. With the end of the Roman control of Europe, various tribes began to fight over the territories; Europe began to move into what was long known as the Dark Ages.

That concept is now generally rejected and the more neutral term Middle Ages suffices. But there is no denying that putting an end to "the ancient world" in A.D. 500 still has a European or Western bias. True, Huns and Mongols began to move into India and across Central Asia about this same time, and people in those lands also experienced difficult times. But not all peoples throughout the world went into a phase of decline. In Central America, for instance, some Mayan centers moved into their classical period; China went through some unsettling years, but by 618 entered a classical period with the Tang dynasty; Islam would prove to be a dynamic force in a large part of the world. Although this volume ends about A.D. 500, it recognizes that peoples outside Europe were still on the move.

Then there are the very words discovery and exploration. Discovery tends to suggest that no one had been there before, and this would hold true for those nameless people who first moved into the various corners of the earth. But the concept of discovery of new lands has come to refer to those who first reported their finds, those who usually returned to their starting points and were the first to write about the lands and peoples they had just visited. Over and over again, this history makes the point that "discovery" depends on a written account.

But this was not necessarily the report of the original discoverer. For that is another characteristic shared by many if not most of these stories of ancient discoveries and explorations: Many of the accounts of ancient discoveries and explorations are secondhand—that is, if there were original firsthand accounts, they were long ago lost, and only reports of the original survive. Furthermore, the accounts are often fragmentary. Much of the evidence comes down to only one record —a passing reference in some text, often one dating from centuries after the alleged event. This often leads scholars—both ancient as well as modern—to question the historical truth of these accounts. This is partly due to the lack of complete documentation of all aspects of the earliest phases of history: Either those ancient peoples did not see fit to record all these stories, or the records did not survive the ravages of the elements and time. In any case, over and over again throughout this book there will be the admission that the true facts about the explorers and their journeys must remain somewhat in question.

There is another reason that these ancient peoples' voyages are sometimes not recognized as discoveries and explorations: They did not have much deliberate concern for or conscious awareness of opening up the world for posterity, for all humankind. The individuals or expeditions went forth to gain some advantage for their sponsors—usually rulers, and neither the explorers nor the sponsors showed much interest in assembling objective knowledge and making it available to the world at large. In fact, knowledge of new places was often jealously guarded for fear that other people might try to gain access to the land and its resources. Rather than give true reports, the first people to discover new lands often circulated stories of wild creatures and dangerous features to frighten off others.

The ancient Phoenicians were particularly notorious for guarding their knowledge of new routes and locales and resources. They wanted to maintain a monopoly in the trade of tin, for example, which they imported from the British Isles. There is even a story recounted by the ancient Greek historian Strabo of a Phoenician ship captain who realized he was being followed by a Roman ship while he was making his way to the British Isles to get a load of tin. Rather than reveal the source of the tin, the Phoenician deliberately led the Roman ship onto a shoal where both ships were wrecked. After he made his way back to the Phoenician colony at Gades, Spain, the captain was rewarded by the government for his loss.

There was one ancient people, though, who stand out as exceptions to most of these practices. A people who showed an interest in the earth other than what it might yield in commercial exploitation. Who did attempt to gather facts about the world beyond their own immediate spheres of trade and power. Above all, who wrote down and circulated as much information as they could about the world, both known and unknown. That people was the ancient Greeks.

Yet not even the ancient Greeks, with a few exceptions, set out deliberately for the sake of "pure" discovery and exploration. And that raises the issue of just what is meant by explorers. In the strict sense, it is intended to identify an individual who consciously sets out primarily to find places unknown at least to large numbers of people and then to make these places known, probably through some written account. In fact, as will become apparent almost from the beginnings of recorded history, many people now credited as "explorers" set out with quite different goals. Especially in the ancient world, most of the voyages and expeditions involved peoples searching for land to possess, for natural resources (often metals) to exploit, and for trade markets to develop. Others were undertaken simply to encourage better diplomatic relations—although again, probably with an eye on increasing trade. And some were really military campaigns, undertaken for conquest.

Yet many of the individuals who conducted these expeditions have come to be honored as explorers. Just as eventually individuals with still other goals—a desire for glory, a love of excitement and danger, a wish to convert others to some religious faith, or even just the sheer pleasure of travel—are honored as explorers.

Because the history of ancient exploration is by definition a subject that has been around for a long time, it is not one that lends itself to much scholarly revision or debate or controversy. There are continual discussions of details at the edges of the subject, but no major scholarly revisions. Many of the debates about ancient exploration, for that matter, have been going on even since ancient times. Questions of the trustworthiness of certain accounts, debates over whether certain claims can be accepted—these can be found in some of the oldest texts about voyages and journeys.

It is interesting to note, in that respect, that the standard histories of the subject today have been around for many decades. Henry Tozer's A History of Ancient Geography was first published in 1897—and continues to be constantly republished. Cary and Warmington's The Ancient Explorers was first published in 1929. H. E. Burton's Discovery of the Ancient World was published in 1932, and J. Oliver Thomson's History of Ancient Geography was published in 1948. They do not differ much from one another, and all the articles and encyclopedia entries (and now Web sites) for the general public tend pretty much to draw on these works. Unlike many phases in the history of exploration that do provoke constant investigation and controversy, there is little of this among serious scholars of the ancient world. The ancient world might be characterized as a "finite" system.

There is, however, another side to the story of ancient exploration that has come alive in relatively recent years and that does seem to provide constant debate, even excitement. And because it is the kind of excitement that is most apt to appeal to young people, it deserves some recognition here. This is the aspect of exploration that confuses the scholarly and authoritative uncertainties about the history of discovery and exploration with exaggerated claims for the possible or imaginative or fabulous. Thus there are claims of searches and discoveries of vanished civilizations and peoples of ancient times—Atlantis and Mu and such places. There are claims of visitors from outer space or supernatural beings who have once inhabited parts of the earth.

Above all, there are the claims for all the peoples who "discovered" the Americas hundreds and even thousands of years before Columbus arrived there. Just limiting the candidates to people from the ancient world, these include: Atlanteans (people from Lost Atlantis), Assyrians, Basque, Canaanites, Catalans, Celts, Chinese, Cro-Magnons, Egyptians, Etruscans, Gauls, Greeks, Hindus, Huns, Israelites (the Lost Tribes), Lemurians (from the lost continent of Mu), Libyans, Madagascans, ancestral Mormons, Phoenicians, Romans, Scythians, Tartars, Trojans, and Welsh. The proponents of these peoples offer all kinds of "evidence," from inscriptions and coins to linguistic and cultural similarities, and their claims appear in an endless stream of articles and books, on the Internet, and even on reputable TV programs. Sometimes the cases are presented in "fuzzy" ways that, although not making an explicit or absolute claim to be true, would leave uninformed minds thinking that, "Well, it must be true." This is especially so when these claims are accompanied by vivid illustrations and apparently authoritative "experts" promoting these claims.

Now these claims are not to be confused with the openly admitted fabulous and imaginative tales of voyages and journeys. These are as old as the earliest literature—indeed, some of the oldest texts known involve just such fabulous journeys, some of which this book discusses. Nor should these modern claims be confused with true scholarly differences or debates. Thus, not all authorities to this day agree on exactly when the first human beings crossed over into the Americas. Not all authorities agree on what lands are referred to in ancient Egyptian texts. Not all authorities agree on whether all the voyages described in ancient Greek texts can be taken literally. A healthy skepticism is the nature of true scholarship, and it is a theme of this book that it can be instructive to be aware of this kind of uncertainty and debate.

Moreover, because these popular claims are so readily available in the media these days—on TV and the Internet, in particular—and because they clearly do catch the attention of young people, this history takes account of them and, wherever relevant, discusses these fabulous ancient tales of Lost Atlantis, of pre-Columbian visitors to the Americas, of questionable Chinese travelers' journeys. It takes them seriously so that readers can understand the difference between dubious claims and true knowledge.

Some of these questionable claims are treated in the short essays in the boxes, or sidebars, a feature of this book designed expressly to discuss topics that supplement the main narrative. Maps, of course, are indispensable in any presentation of discovery and exploration, which by their very nature involve geography, land and seas. Specially created maps are provided to show clearly all the major areas and routes. Illustrations, too, help to provide a more physical dimension to the subject matter. Here a somewhat special problem arises because there are no contemporary pictures of the ancient explorers or ships or events discussed. Considerable effort has been made, however, to gather as many relevant illustrations as possible—some especially taken for this book. Yet another special dimension to any discussion of the ancient world is that the subject involves foreign peoples and cultures, and so many unfamiliar terms and words must be used. The glossary provides a handy way to remain constantly aware of the meanings of these words.

Finally, to aid those who would like to follow up on any of the topics—which inevitably in a book such as this can be discussed relatively briefly—the "Further Information" section offers a list of books that might be consulted for more detailed presentations. And it includes not only works of nonfiction.

It has long been accepted that good novels can sometimes capture the true flavor of historical periods, events, and personages as well if not better than nonfiction, so the list includes a selection of some of the better novels dealing at least peripherally with these matters. There are now many excellent documentaries and educational films about subjects in this book, and the list provides the names of a number of the more relevant films available on videos (and now DVDs). Also, recognizing that many people today enjoy obtaining their information from the Internet, the list provides a selection of some of the more informative sites. There are scores more Web sites, but as indicated above, in referring to the claims made for all kinds of fanciful explorers, the Internet must be used judiciously.

One of the goals of this book, in fact, is to convince readers that the true story of discovery and exploration in the ancient world is at least as fascinating as those wild claims. In leading readers along this exciting narrative trail, the book's ultimate goal is to give them the sense of making their own journey of discovery and exploration.

1

PYTHEAS VOYAGES NORTH

About 315 B.C., Pytheas, a citizen of the Greek colony of Massalia, on the Mediterranean coast of France, headed his ship westward to the Pillars of Hercules. This was the ancient Greeks' name for the Strait of Gibraltar, the body of water between Gibraltar and North Africa. (A Greek myth claimed that Hercules had placed two rocks to guard the strait.) To pass through this strait at that period of history was a major undertaking by a ship captain: It meant heading for the uncharted waters

The Rock of Gibraltar, just off the south coast of Spain, was considered by the ancient Greeks as one of the Pillars of Hercules, beyond which lay the ocean largely unknown to ancient Mediterranean mariners and generally regarded as a mysterious region. *(Library of Congress, Prints and Photographs Division [LC-USZ62-108739])*

The old port of Marseilles, France, here seen in a late 19th-century photo, might well have looked somewhat like this about 315 B.C. when it was known as Massalia and Pytheas sailed from it and headed for the Atlantic Ocean. *(Library of Congress, Prints and Photographs Division [LC-DIG-ppmsc-05118])*

and unknown lands of the North Atlantic region. But Pytheas had set his sights on just such a voyage.

Even before he reached the Pillars of Hercules, Pytheas faced potential dangers. Massalia had been founded about 600 B.C. by Greeks from the city of Phocea on the coast of Asia Minor (modern Foca, in Turkey) and in the centuries since had grown and prospered as a center of Greek culture and commerce in the western Mediterranean. Located just east of the mouth of the Rhone River, Massalia served as an entrepôt, or trading center, for merchants from all over the Mediterranean and merchants who came down the Rhone from northwestern Europe.

Carthaginians were an assertive people, determined to dominate the maritime traffic and commerce in the western Mediterranean. (Within 50 years the Carthaginians would be fighting Rome for mastery of the western Mediterranean.) Carthaginians had established their own colonies along the coast of Spain, and they did not take kindly to the Greeks who also wanted a share of the commerce.

In particular, their colony of Gades (modern Cadiz), on the coast of Spain just outside the Pillars of Hercules, was positioned to cut off Greeks or others who might seek to sail out of the Mediterranean. Pytheas made his way along the south coast of France, down the east coast of Spain, through the Pillars of Hercules, and then along the southern coast of Spain and Portugal. He must have been very clever or lucky to avoid any conflict with Carthaginians because ships in those days sailed and rowed quite close to the coast during the day.

Pytheas's ship, by the way, was most likely a merchant, or cargo, ship, not a warship. Those were the two major types of ships at this time. Warships were designed for speed and strength and were relatively shallow, long, and trim; they were propelled by many oarsmen. This type of ship would not have been practical for a long voyage. Merchant ships were designed to hold cargo and so were deeper, broader, and sturdy; most were propelled by one large sail attached to a central mast, but some merchant ships also had several oarsmen on each side. Both warships and merchant ships were steered mainly by large oars at the stern, or the rear, of the ships.

For a journey as ambitious as that of Pytheas, his ship probably had oarsmen—perhaps 10 on each side. His total crew may have been about 30 men. The oarsmen enabled the ship to make some progress during the hours when there was no favorable wind. Even so, the ship probably only averaged about five or six miles

During those same centuries, another city on the opposite shore of the Mediterranean had also grown powerful and prosperous. This was Carthage, on the coast of North Africa (modern Tunisia) almost due south of Massalia. Carthage had been founded about 750 B.C. by Phoenicians from the eastern coast of the Mediterranean—modern Lebanon. The

Ancient Navigation

In the thousands of years before Pytheas that humans had been sailing the open seas, and for at least another 1,500 years, the knowledge, skills, and devices used for navigating ships hardly changed. Most mariners basically depended on *dead reckoning*—estimates of their location at sea based on some sense of a distance traveled and the time elapsed, modified by such matters as position of the sun and the strength of the winds. Furthermore, they depended on a store of common knowledge (e.g., familiar landmarks, the rising and setting of the sun, and the positions of certain stars and planets).

In the Mediterranean, except for coastal trips, most ship traffic ceased by about November 1 and did not start in again until April: Ship owners and crews simply did not want to take the risk of running into foul weather. Even during the sailing months, ships never needed to be much more than 150 miles from shore. But at an average of five knots an hour, that was still a solid 30-hour trip, and that meant sailing at night and navigating by the stars. Although experienced navigators knew how to do this, most ships pulled into shore or at least safe harbors at night.

Knowing familiar landmarks such as promontories or cliffs or populated sites and human constructions was not enough: Navigators had to know what the

---

an hour, so that on a long day they might cover some 50 miles. The energy expended on keeping such a ship moving must have required a fair amount of calories and liquids for the crew, so they had to pull their ship ashore each night to replenish their food and water supplies.

THE JOURNEY

Once past the southwestern corner of the Iberian Peninsula, Pytheas sailed northward along the Atlantic coast of Portugal and northwestern Spain. Arriving at the Bay of Biscay, he almost certainly stayed fairly close to the coast of France until he arrived at the great promontory of Brittany. Proceeding along it, he reached the island of Ushant, the westernmost territory of modern France. At that point

he had to make one of his longest "runs" in the open sea—some 100 miles, a solid 24-hour trip, to reach the southwestern coast of England. Once there he proceeded to the region known to him as Belerion, today known as Land's End, the promontory of Cornwall, England's southwesternmost region.

Pytheas may not have been the first Mediterranean mariner to have sailed this route, although he would be the first to provide a written report of many of the features of the coast. (The book he wrote has never been found, but during the following centuries many ancient writers quoted from it.) When Pytheas reached England, his voyage becomes a major contribution to the history of exploration. The people of the Mediterranean had only the vaguest notion of the lands in northwestern Europe, especially the

possible hazards were when approaching shore—reefs, rocks, treacherous currents. All such knowledge was learned by experience and then passed on by word of mouth.

The document known as a *periplus*—literally, a "sailing around"—was little more than a list of places along the coast and would not come into use until about 500 B.C. Likewise, the astrolabe—an instrument that could be used to find the latitude—although it may have been invented by about 200 B.C., did not come into general use for many centuries later.

Probably the only instrument or device that these early navigators used was a sounding rod, or line. To measure the depth of the water at any given point, they dropped down a line with a lead weight until it hit bottom. The more sophisticated lead weights had a little hollow at the bottom that was filled with tallow or grease. When it was brought to the surface, it revealed the nature of the ocean floor at that point, and experienced navigators could tell a lot from this.

In the Greek language, the helmsman of a ship who also served as the navigator was known as a *kybernetes*—"governor." This became the root of the modern word *cybernetics*—the science of control and communications processes, and this in turn has provided the prefix, *cyber-* for any number of words involving "navigation" by computers. So it is that today's most advanced technology links itself to the basic but intelligent skills of ancient navigation.

islands later to be known as the British Isles. What they did know, though, is that a particular material came from somewhere in that region: tin.

Tin was among the scarcest and most valued products sought by the peoples of the Mediterranean. For some 3,000 years, they had been mixing tin with copper to form a durable alloy, bronze. Bronze was used for making everything from weapons to religious objects, from armor to jewelry, from tools to coins, from statues to drinking vessels. Copper was relatively plentiful around the Mediterranean, but tin was obtainable from only a few sources. For some centuries, tin had been imported into the Mediterranean region from northwestern Spain and the British Isles. After being extracted from its rocky ore, the metal was transported overland through Spain or France to the shores of the Mediterranean.

Massalia was one of the major trading centers for tin, but most of the Mediterraneans involved in this trade had little knowledge of its places of origin. They were dependent on the middlemen who transferred it from its source, and this added considerably to the price. There were rumors of rich tin mines on islands in that northern ocean; indeed, the Greeks' word for "tin," *kassiteros,* had been given to the distant islands believed to be the source of tin, the Cassiterides. Evidently some of the merchants of Massalia wanted to make direct contact with those miners, and that seems to have been one of the chief goals of Pytheas's expedition— to find those tin mines. When Pytheas arrived at the islands off Cornwall, he was convinced he had found that place.

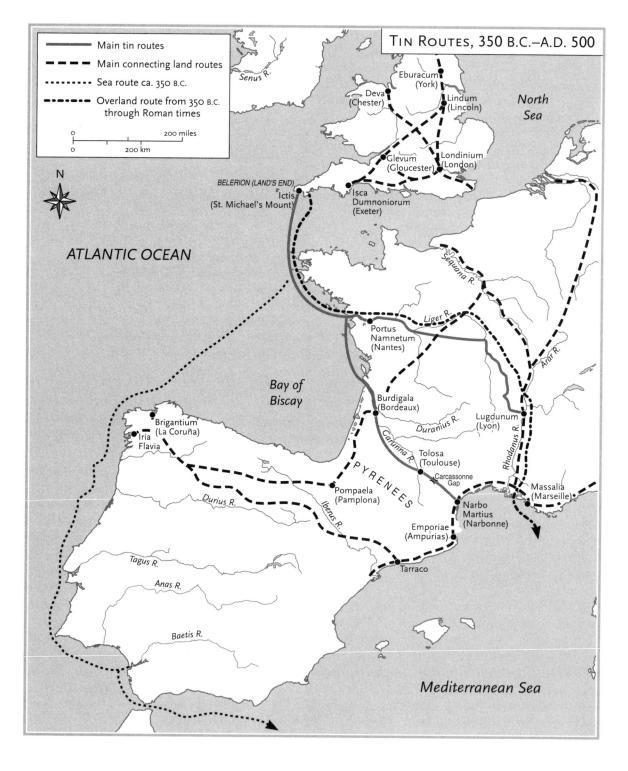

TIN ROUTES, 350 B.C.–A.D. 500

Main tin routes
Main connecting land routes
Sea route ca. 350 B.C.
Overland route from 350 B.C. through Roman times

0   200 miles
0   200 km

N

Senus R.

North Sea

Eburacum (York)
Deva (Chester)
Lindum (Lincoln)
Glevum (Gloucester)
Londinium (London)

BELERION (LAND'S END)
Ictis (St. Michael's Mount)
Isca Dumnoniorum (Exeter)

ATLANTIC OCEAN

Sequana R.

Liger R.

Arar R.

Portus Namnetum (Nantes)

Bay of Biscay

Burdigala (Bordeaux)

Lugdunum (Lyon)

Duranius R.

Rhodanus R.

Brigantium (La Coruña)
Iria Flavia

Garunna R.

Tolosa (Toulouse)
Carcassonne Gap

Massalia (Marseille)

P Y R E N E E S

Pompaela (Pamplona)

Durius R.

Ibenus R.

Emporiae (Ampurias)

Narbo Martius (Narbonne)

Tagus R.

Anas R.

Tarraco

Baetis R.

Mediterranean Sea

In fact, he soon discovered that the tin mines were on the mainland of Cornwall, and Pytheas would describe the process:

> They extract the tin from its bed by a cunning process. The bed is of rock, but contains earthy interstices, along which they cut a gallery. Having melted the tin and refined it, they hammer it into knucklebone shape and convey it to an adjacent island named Ictis [possibly St. Michael's Mount off the coast of Cornwall].

Having satisfied himself that he had found the source of the tin—and possibly loaded his boat with some—Pytheas then sailed completely around Great Britain. His reported measurement of the coastline—based on estimates of the length of land passed in his daily voyage—was surprisingly exact, and he got one thing right: "Britain is triangular like Sicily, with three unequal sides." And he did more than sail along the coast; although most scholars cannot accept his claim that "I traversed the whole of Britannike accessible by foot," he does seem to have made occasional visits into the interior, and he reported on the people he encountered:

> The inhabitants of Britain are said to have sprung from the soil and to preserve a primitive style of life. They make use of chariots in war, such as the ancient Greek heroes are reputed to have employed in the Trojan War; and their habitations are rough-and-

St. Michael's Mount lies just off Cornwall, the southwestern tip of England, and is considered by some scholars to be the isle of Ictis that Pytheas referred to as the port from which tin was shipped. *(Library of Congress, Prints and Photographs Division [LC-DIG-ppmsc-08234])*

The monumental Stonehenge on Salisbury Plain in southwestern England is thought to date from at least 1900 B.C., but there is no suggestion that Pytheas was even aware of it. Exactly who built it and why is not known, but some reputable scholars believe it was built by practitioners of the Druidic religion who may have used it to make astronomical calculations to time their observances. *(© Philip Baird www.anthroarcheart.org)*

ready, being for the most part constructed of wattles or logs. . . . They are simple in their habits and far removed from the cunning and knavishness of modern man.

When he reached the northern coast of Scotland, he was told about the island of Thule, which he claimed was six days' sail north of Britain. He did not venture that far, but he did report that around Thule "there is neither sea nor air but a mixture like sea-lung, in which earth and air are suspended." Exactly what he meant by "sea-lung" would never be known for sure; some say he was describing jellyfish, some say slush-ice, but very likely he was describing the thick, clammy fogs of the North Atlantic. He also described large fish blowing out sprays of water—obviously whales. As for Thule itself, some claim it is Iceland, others Norway, still others the Shetland Islands. In any case, he also reported that Thule was so far north that, in the middle of

summer, the sun went down for only two or three hours. In general, much of what Pytheas would describe and report was a mixture of the truth and misunderstanding.

After completing his encirclement of Britain, Pytheas returned across the Channel to the coast of France or Belgium, then sailed north along the coasts of the Netherlands and Germany. Exactly how far northeastward he sailed is not known, for the names he assigned to the geographic features he saw cannot be attached with any certainty to known features today. But it does appear he moved into the North Sea, possibly as far as the mouth of the Elbe River, where he probably turned back when he confronted the great peninsula topped by Denmark.

In any case, he retraced his voyage home by sticking close to the coast of western Europe and appears to have arrived safely home in Massalia. His journey had covered some 7,500 miles, longer than Christopher

N

PYTHEAS'S VOYAGE, CA. 315 B.C.

ICELAND

ATLANTIC OCEAN

Faroes

NORWAY

Shetlands

Outer
Hebrides

*Orcades
(Orkneys)*

*North
Sea*

Jutland

HIERIYO
(IRELAND)

ALBION
(BRITAIN)

Belerion

ARMORICA
(Brittany)

Nantes

Burdigala

ALPES   MARITIMES

GALACIA

SIERRA MORENO

Emporion

Massalia

Corsica

Rome

TARTESSOS

Gades

Balearic Is.

Sardinia

Pilllars of
Hercules

Mediterranean Sea

Carthage

Sicily

Commonly accepted route

Possible alternative routes

0   400 miles

0   400 km

Columbus's roundtrips to the New World. But unlike Columbus's voyage, what happened as a result of Pytheas's voyage is unknown. There is no evidence of much of anything changing in the tin trade, for instance. As for Pytheas, he vanishes from history. Even the book or report he wrote about his voyage did not survive in its original copy.

THE SIGNIFICANCE OF PYTHEAS

Nothing is known about Pytheas before or after his voyage. He is known only from allu-

sions to him and quotations attributed to him by several ancient Greek and Roman writers—primarily Diodorus Siculus (fl. 60–20 B.C.), Strabo (ca. 63 B.C.–A.D. ca. 24), and Pliny the Elder (A.D. 23–79). Ironically, several of the ancients who describe Pytheas regarded him as a liar—that is, they did not believe he had made the voyage or discovered the things he described. Although some of these ancient writers quote long passages from the report written by Pytheas—it is these secondhand quotations that have been cited here—no part of the original has survived. This in itself is not that unusual: There are many famous individ-

---

The *Kyrenia*
AN ANCIENT SHIP SALVAGED

There is a ship dating from about the time of Pytheas that actually exists to this day. In 1967, a Greek-Cypriot sponge-diver was diving in the Mediterranean off the coast of Kyrenia, Cyprus, when he saw on the sea bottom what looked like the wreck of a ship and its cargo. Ancient shipwrecks have been found elsewhere in the Mediterranean before and since, but they yielded only small remains and incomplete knowledge. By the time skilled underwater archaeologists had raised the "Kyrenian ship," they had salvaged what was not only the oldest Greek vessel discovered to that time but also the best-preserved ship of the classical Greek world. Using the most advanced methods known, they were able to save almost 75 percent of the ship because its wood was fairly well preserved under a layer of sand.

The ship, made of Aleppo pine, was some 47 feet long and 14 feet wide. It was a merchant ship, and its cargo included about 400 amphorae, the large clay urns used throughout the Mediterranean to ship wine and oil. On this ship, the urns were evidently also storing almonds. Stone querns, or large grinding stones, were found, as were bronze coins. In the bow of the ship were recovered some plates, bowls, ladles, sieves, a copper cauldron, salt dishes, oil jugs, cups and wooden spoons; it is assumed they belonged to the crew. After scientific dating of the various elements, scientists determined that the ship sank about 290 B.C. but was built about a century before that.

The *Kyrenia,* as it came to be called, after the wood was treated in such a way that preserved it, was reconstructed in a museum in Kyrenia, Cyprus, where all

uals from the ancient world about whom nothing is known except from references in various texts. But there are enough consistent references to Pytheas that modern scholars are convinced such a man did exist. All who wrote about Pytheas located him in Massalia, and they seem to place his voyage sometime between 325 and 305 B.C. His name suggests he was a Greek, and he was almost certainly of Greek descent, but considering that the Greeks had been settled in Massalia since about 600 B.C., and that various other peoples lived in the immediate environs, he may well have been of mixed heritage.

If so little is known of the man, why do all who write about the beginnings of exploration in the ancient world devote so many words to Pytheas? Why does he stand as an archetypal figure of the explorer?

Some of the ancient texts suggest that Pytheas was a relatively poor man, that he was of no great distinction, but simply undertook the voyage as a commercial venture. It then has been suggested that he must have had the backing of wealthier merchants in Massalia who wanted Pytheas to locate the exact sources of tin so they could purchase this directly and so outmaneuver the

the artifacts found with it are also to be seen. In 1985, a replica, named *Kyrenia II*, was launched in Piraeus, Greece, and in 1987 sailed from Cyprus to Greece on a trial run voyage. The ship endured two storms but completed the journey in 20 days. Since then it has sailed at various events around the world, including the centennial celebration of the Statue of Liberty in New York City in 1986.

The *Kyrenia* probably differed considerably from Pytheas's ship because it was not designed for a long voyage on the ocean, but it remains an amazing survivor of that period of maritime history.

This ancient Greek vase is a distinctive type, the amphora; relatively large, its two handles allowed a person to pour out wine or other liquids. For transporting wine at sea, plain clay amphorae were used. This one, for domestic use, is in the black-figured style, with black figures on the light background— here depicting a shoemaker's shop. *(Library of Congress, Prints and Photographs Division [LC-USZ62-107428])*

Carthaginians in their attempt to monopolize the tin trade. Not only that, the Massalians might then eliminate the middlemen involved in the overland route down across France.

In any case, it seems almost certain that Pytheas must have been at least partially motivated by the prospects of profit. If not a prosperous merchant himself, he must have appreciated what lay in store for him should he complete such a voyage. At the same time, it is highly unlikely that a poor man could ever have been able to finance the ship and crew necessary for such an expedition. So if he was relatively poor, he must have had enough of a reputation that the merchants of Massalia supported him.

Whoever he was, whatever motivated him to undertake such a voyage, he must have been a master mariner. Sailing a ship for thousands of miles in those days was no easy feat—most ships never sailed that far from their home ports. Although the Mediterranean Sea extended some 2,200 miles from the eastern shores to the Pillars of Hercules and 600 miles at its widest, most ships at this time would never have considered trying to sail to such distant shores. They loaded and unloaded their cargoes at various intermediate ports. In any case, they put into familiar and safe harbors at night. They never ventured that far from coasts, and they knew the various landmarks. When navigational skills were called for, they knew the winds, they knew the stars, they knew the dangers lurking beneath the waves. But Pytheas sailed into completely unknown, uncharted seas. There were no maps or charts, no familiar landmarks, no way to know about the reefs or rocks as he approached a shore. He had to be a master mariner, a master navigator.

Some of those who wrote about him, in addition to referring to him as a master mariner, treated him as a serious astronomer.

They credited him with asserting—rightfully—that there was no star precisely over the North Pole. At least one ancient text that referred to him said that he set off on his voyage to confirm this claim. He was one of the first known people to have connected the influence of the moon to the rise and fall of the tides. Also, by carefully calculating the changing position of the sun and the resultant length of shadows, he was able to calculate the latitude of Massalia quite accurately. On his voyage, he also recorded the lengthening of the days as they proceeded northward, and by observing the height of the Sun, he calculated the latitude at various points along the way. Many geographers and mapmakers who followed Pytheas used his latitude for Massalia as the basis for calculating the latitudes of other points in the known world.

There was another skill that Pytheas must have had. It was not enough to guide a ship safely through hundreds of miles of ocean. The ship had a crew—exactly how many is not known, but most likely about 30, including oarsmen, sail crew, and officers. These men had to be provided with adequate food and drink, day after day. They put into shore every night and probably often stayed several days while they replenished their food supplies—sending out hunting parties and water seekers. Men probably got sick or injured. His ship must have occasionally required repairs. Often he had to deal with the native inhabitants. He probably carried some valuable cargo that he could use as barter, that is, to trade for vital supplies. So Pytheas had to be a good administrator of such an expedition. This meant not just satisfying material needs. He must have been a good leader of men, someone who could inspire his crew to keep going, to persevere against all odds.

In recent times, some speak of Pytheas as though he was a lone adventurer, setting out to explore for the sake of exploration, for the sheer sake of revealing the unknown, of finding what lay back of beyond. That is probably too modern a notion of such a man and such an expedition. But there had to be something of the adventurer in Pytheas. No one could have forced him to undertake such a voyage. Meanwhile, there must have been hundreds, even thousands of mariners in Massalia who did *not* choose to go. He had to have some special spark, some special vision. And he certainly had to have courage—the willingness to set forth into the unknown, the guts to face all that nature and humans might throw at him. Physical strength, too: Although there might have been an element of good luck for men of his era to survive and endure, Pytheas must have overcome hardships of many kinds: storms at sea, cold and wetness, lack of proper foods, and occasional accidents and injuries.

It turns out, then, that Pytheas must have combined in himself many of the main elements that will be found in explorers not only in the ancient world but also in explorers across the ages and of all cultures. Not all explorers had all these qualities and characteristics and skills, but they had to have some of them. Some would be driven primarily by the profit motive, often expressed as a desire to seek gold. But even if they had that personal goal, many like Pytheas needed to gain the support of others, whether fellow seekers after personal profit or rulers who wanted the profits for their realms. Like Pytheas, almost all explorers had to have the knowledge and skills either to navigate ships or conduct expeditions across unknown terrain. They had to be able to organize the logistics of an expedition—provide the food and shelter needed, maintain the ships or the animals. They had to be able to inspire their "teams," to hold the members of their expeditions together through thick and thin. Some explorers, it is

true, were motivated by an almost pure desire for understanding the world—advancing the sciences, adding to knowledge, enlarging the known. But all must have had some sense of adventure. Even the most scientific of explorers had to have something that took them out of the library or the laboratory to set forth and confront unknown physical challenges. So all had to have some form of courage. Possibly, too, they had a touch of ego to think that they could carry off what lesser men might not be up to undertaking.

Finally, what links Pytheas to many of the great explorers who followed, but distinguishes him from most who went before him, is that he does seem to have written an account of his voyage. He was wrong about many of the details he described. He was not believed by many of his contemporaries. But the point was that he brought these dim and distant lands into the light of human awareness. It was not enough to travel bravely to distant lands. Unless some record was made, some report, even contemporaries would not know for certain what lay out there, and posterity would definitely not know. There have been explorers who have personally shown little or no interest in recording their discoveries or their own role in daring expeditions. But one way or another, someone must set down an account for the world to profit, to add to its steadily enlarging realm of the known.

Most explorers before Pytheas did not record their adventures, but this does not mean that the world had not been explored. Clearly there were people living all over the earth by the time Pytheas made his voyage of "discovery." Before giving credit to the many brave explorers known to have preceded and followed Pytheas, it seems necessary to recognize the many anonymous and unsung people who were truly the first to open up the world.

2

THE ORIGINAL EXPLORERS

Pytheas, the ancient Greek mariner who figures so prominently in histories of exploration, was by no means the first person to travel in the regions he explored. Rather, he owes his fame to the fact that he wrote about his voyage, and so brought his activities into the light of history. But there is another lesson that such a voyage of "discovery" brings to the fore: The lands Pytheas visited and explored were inhabited.

This is true for many if not most of the individuals honored as "discoverers" and explorers throughout history. They were not the first human beings to be present in the lands and waters associated with their names and feats. This is as true of the oldest known ancient explorers as with the 20th century's great explorers. Except for expeditions in the polar regions and space, most explorers have been going into regions already inhabited or traveled—perhaps not completely or densely populated, perhaps not frequently or thoroughly traveled. But human beings had long been settled throughout many parts of the world before writing began to record the names of explorers for history.

The *ancient world*, as mentioned previously, is usually defined as beginning with the first appearance of writing. This major threshold in human culture differs for various regions of the world, but it does tend to appear about the same time in many places—about 3500 to 3000 B.C. That is when writing or at least characters, symbols, or drawings of some kind appear to be recording information.

Before that time is what is known as *prehistory,* and tools, bones, hearth remains, and other kinds of physical evidence are needed to trace the presence of human beings for this period. At that point, archaeologists and physical anthropologists usually take over from historians. They are the ones who find out when and where human beings first appeared. And it can be argued that it is these first human beings in each part of the world who deserve to be known as the first discoverers and explorers.

THE EARLIEST EXPLORERS

The earliest ancestors of human beings are classified as hominids, and virtually all authorities agree that the hominids emerged in East and South Africa. Depending on the characteristics that scientists and others require to define a "human being," the first primitive ancestors known as *Homo erectus* ("erect man") appeared about 1.8 million years ago. Not long after that, these primitive beings began to show up in places far removed from their original sites, specifically in China, India, and Java. (Some even claim that *Homo erectus* remains are found in Japan.) Again, most experts believe that these primitive hominids made their way up Africa's east coast, across Egypt—or somehow crossed

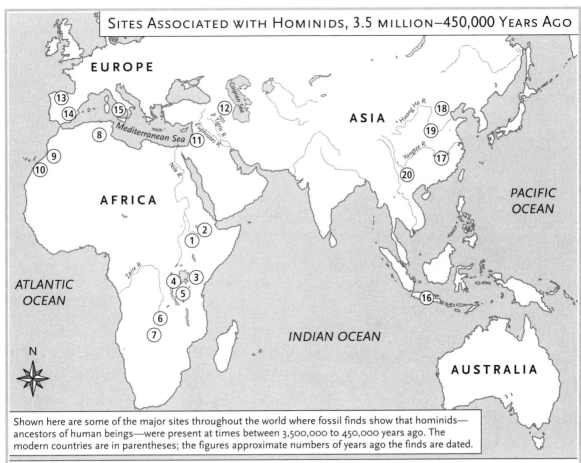

SITES ASSOCIATED WITH HOMINIDS, 3.5 MILLION–450,000 YEARS AGO

Shown here are some of the major sites throughout the world where fossil finds show that hominids—ancestors of human beings—were present at times between 3,500,000 to 450,000 years ago. The modern countries are in parentheses; the figures approximate numbers of years ago the finds are dated.

1. Hadar (Ethiopia) 3,200,000
2. Gona (Ethiopia) 2,550,000
3. Turkana (Kenya) 1,600,000
4. Olduvai (Tanzania) 1,850,000
5. Laetoli (Tanzania) 3,500,000
6. Swartkrans (South Africa) 1,500,000
7. Sterkfontein (South Africa) 2,000,000

8. Ternifine (Algeria) 600,000
9. Sidi Abdettahman (Morocco) 600,000
10. Thomas Quarries (Morocco) 600,000
11. Ubeidiya (Israel) 1,400,000
12. Dmanisi (Georgia) 1,800,000
13. Atapuerca (Spain) 780,000
14. Orce (Spain) 1,000,000

15. Ceprano (Italy) 800,000
16. Java (Indonesia) 1,200,000
17. Longgpu (China) 1,800,000
18. Zhoukoudian (China) 450,000
19. Lantien (China) 800,00
20. Yuanmou (China) 600,000

the narrowest straits of the Red Sea and the Persian Gulf—and then wandered all the way across Asia. Until relatively recently, it was not thought that such early beings moved all the way into Europe, but sites such as those in the Sierra de Atapurca and Orce, Spain, and Ceprano, Italy, have yielded human fossils and other remains indicating that *Homo erectus* was present as early as 1 million years ago.

Why such creatures would have traveled so far and in different directions can probably never be known. But something motivated these hominids to keep pushing forward, to move ever onward into unknown territory. Perhaps this instinct, this drive, is what distin-

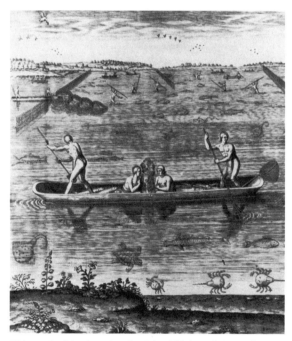

Although this drawing by John White of Roanoke Indians in a dugout canoe dates to the late 1580s, it is assumed that some of the earliest watercraft made by humans were not unlike this—crude boats made from hollowed-out tree trunks—and used to travel to islands such as Australia. *(Library of Congress, Prints and Photographs Division [LC-USZ62-54016])*

guishes them both as humans themselves and as ancestors of later humans.

The next major stage of human evolution occurred between about 500,000 to 160,000 years ago, when the Archaic *Homo sapiens* ("wise man") appeared, first in Africa but, within 30,000 years, also in China, India, the Middle East, Central Asia, and Europe. Experts do not agree on whether these ancestors of modern *Homo sapiens* evolved independently in each of these regions or whether they came from some single group of migrants. In either case, these people clearly moved into previously uninhabited areas. Their physical remains are found across Europe, from England to Greece, in remote parts of Uzbekistan, and throughout eastern China. Whatever their origins, whatever their motivation, these people were opening up new lands.

Then, by at least 130,000 years ago, the anatomically modern species known as *Homo sapiens sapiens* appeared. This is the species that all human beings today belong to. The oldest known fossils have been found in Africa, but similar fossils almost as old— sometimes designated Archaic *Homo sapiens* —have been found in other parts of the Old World, and this has led to two competing theories. One of them, sometimes called the "Out of Africa Hypothesis," claims that the new species evolved in Africa and about 55,000 years ago migrated up to the Middle East; some individuals then split off and went over into India and Southeast Asia and East Asia. Others went up into Central Asia and from there split into groups, one at least going west into Europe, another heading farther east into northeastern Asia. As they moved, this new species displaced any local populations of Archaic *Homo sapiens*.

The other theory, sometimes known as "The Regional Continuity Hypothesis," claims that the *Homo sapiens sapiens* in each region

Homo sapiens as *Homo explorans*

The English word *explorer* comes from the Latin word, *explorare*, which in turn was based on the Latin meaning "to cry out," a reference, it is believed, to hunters calling out when they had sighted game. The proposal to characterize the human species as *Homo explorans*, "the human as explorer," thus turns out to recognize that the first "explorers" were very likely the men who went out in search of game. This motive for the forward movement of human populations into ever more distant regions has been accepted for some time by anthropologists and other students of the earliest human beings. Some of the most convincing evidence that the earliest human beings were present in remote places of the earth are animal bones with signs of having been broken or scraped in a manner indicating someone was eating the flesh off these bones.

The theory has been that even the earliest ancestors of modern humans who moved out of Africa were searching for more plentiful sources of food. They could gather some vegetable matter—fruits, nuts, berries, roots—but this was left to the women and children. For the energy required to survive in a hostile or at least competitive environment, animal meat was needed, and it was men's task to secure it. Since these hunters would understandably want to obtain their prey as easily as possible, it makes sense that they would periodically move on to find more plentiful populations.

An analogy might be what happens to this day in many places where there is a hunting season for particular species—deer or moose or game birds. People who live in these regions often see these wild animals appearing quite frequently and openly when there is no hunting allowed. When the hunting season commences, it seems that these animals are no longer so easy to find. Do the animals know the law? Obviously not, but they do know what the sound of a gun means, and they know what the sound of people thrashing around in the woods can mean. So the animals lie low or move into less accessible areas.

Both the limits of laws and terrain prevent modern hunters from chasing their intended prey ever farther. But there were no such limits on the first human beings. Whether they killed most of the animals in a given area or simply drove them away, the hunters could keep moving on into virgin territory in search of game. If this is true, if this is how the world was discovered and settled, then *Homo explorans*, "the human as explorer," the crier-out at the sight of game, becomes almost synonymous with *Homo sapiens*, the "wise human" who survived to populate the earth.

evolved from the Archaic *Homo sapiens* living in that region. However, even in this theory, all modern humans are fundamentally the same because their common ancestors, the Archaic *Homo sapiens*, were the same. Again, though, whatever the origins of *Homo sapiens sapiens*, they were clearly on the move. Not only did they spread throughout ever-farther parts of the main landmasses of Europe and Asia, they moved into several new regions. In Southeast Asia, for instance, they moved into the lands known today as Burma (Myanmar), Cambodia, Indonesia, Laos, Thailand, and Vietnam. But perhaps even more striking is that they now moved over onto relatively distant islands such as Sri Lanka, the Philippines, and Taiwan. Above all, they moved over onto Australia—at least by 45,000 years ago.

The earth's sea levels were much lower during much of this time, so that some islands of today were in fact linked by land. But Australia and the islands mentioned above were separated by at least 50 miles from the mainland, which means that these first settlers must have had some kind of basic water transport—most likely rafts or crude dugouts. One theory, in fact, is that the *Homo sapiens* who moved from the Middle East to Southeast Asia during many thousands of years had done so by making short boat trips along the coasts. But whether they moved over land or sea, these early *Homo sapiens* were demonstrating physical courage, intelligent thought, and some form of emotional energy in their commitment to moving into new territory.

THE FIRST AMERICANS

Nowhere was this truer than in what was probably the most significant movement in this era—the migration of humans into the Western Hemisphere. Not all authorities agree on the time when these first humans appeared in North America, but it seems that it was at least about 16,000 B.C. Not all authorities agree, either, on the exact people who were the first to come, but most believe they were people living in Siberia or eastern Asia—possibly the ancestors of the Chukchi people of northeast-

ern Siberia, possibly related to people once living in Central Asia. Scholars, however, are increasingly suspecting that at least some individuals from other origins were among the early immigrants to North America.

Finally, not all authorities agree on just how these first settlers in the Americas came—that is, by what route and by what mode of transport. But once again, most authorities believe they came on foot over the land bridge now known as Beringia. For about this time—20,000–12,000 B.C.—the last phase of the great Ice Age still had quantities of the earth's water "locked up" in massive ice caps and glaciers that covered much of North America and northern Eurasia. This meant that the world's sea levels were so low that the land between Siberia and Alaska was exposed, and it was by this route that the first humans entered North America. (Other authorities now believe that at least some of these first Americans made their way by boats from Asia to the western shores of North America.)

As with all these matters of prehistory, there is not total agreement among the experts as to the date of the first appearance of humans in the Americas. There are actually a few experts who claim they have found tools at sites such as Calico, California, dated to as far back as 200,000 years ago: This would mean that Archaic *Homo sapiens* made their way there. Other experts claim to be able to date human bones found at Taber, in Alberta, Canada, and the Yuha Desert of southern California to 50,000 to 25,000 years ago; hearths and stone tools found at Pedra Furada, in northeastern Brazil, to about 48,000 years ago; and tools and other evidence at the Orogrande Cave in New Mexico, to about 30,000 years ago. Such claims, however, are not accepted by most students of this subject.

Then there are a group of sites where the excavators date the human presence to peri-

The excavators of the Meadowcroft Rock Shelter, in Avella, Pennsylvania (near the border of West Virginia), claim that it was inhabited by humans at least by 12,500 B.C., which would make it one of the oldest known such sites in the Western Hemisphere. *(Courtesy of Francesca DiPietro Bowman)*

ods earlier than the most commonly accepted ones but not so much earlier as to be rejected by all experts. Bluefish Cave in Alaska and a site in Venezuela, Taima Taima, have yielded bones with unusual markings that may have been made by humans about 23,000 B.C. At the Pikimachay ("Flea Cave") in the Ayacicho Valley in Peru, an excavator claims to have found tools dating to about 20,000 to 15,000 years ago. At a site known as Monte Verde in Chile, the excavators claim to have evidence that dates the site to about 11,000 B.C. Two of the more intriguing sites excavated only since the 1990s are Meadowcroft Rock Shelter, about

one hour east of Pittsburgh, Pennsylvania, and the Cactus Hill site near Petersburg, Virginia; at both these sites, excavators claim to have found evidence of human occupation that dates back to at least 12,500 B.C. (Because of these early dates now being assigned to finds in the Northeast, there are some experts claiming that at least some of the earliest humans in North America made their way there from western Europe; most authorities reject such claims.)

Although the claims for the dates at these sites remain controversial, virtually all experts agree on the finds dating to about 9500 B.C. as

These spear points, made from a type of stone known as chert, are called Clovis points after the site in New Mexico where the first such were identified. These were found in Colorado, but Clovis points were used by the inhabitants of much of North America between about 9500–8500 B.C. *(Peter Bostrom, National Museum Collection)*

indisputable proof of human presence in the Americas. These people are referred to as Paleo-Indians ("ancient Indians") and are assumed to be the direct ancestors of most of the Indians of the Americas. (They were not, however, the ancestors of the people long named "Eskimos" but now more scientifically called Inuit and Kalaadit; they did not appear in Alaska until about 9000 B.C.) The finds are the stone weapons known as Clovis points, named after the site in New Mexico where they were first found in 1929, and were attached to spears. Clovis points were used throughout North America—indicating not

just a widespread population but a shared way of life, one based on hunting the megafauna, or large animals that then roamed the Americas: mammoths and mastodons, giant bison and yaks, saber-toothed lions, large wolves, ground sloths, and camels. By about 8500 B.C., the Clovis point was replaced by a slightly different stone spear point known as the Folsom point (also after the site in New Mexico where first found, in 1927). It is believed that the Folsom people were then hunting the large bison in the West and the caribou in the East.

Whether the oldest and most controversial dates are true or only the universally accepted dates of the Clovis and Folsom cultures are true is not the issue here. Rather, what is truly remarkable about the appearance of the first human beings in the Western Hemisphere is how fast they moved down and throughout the Americas. For instance, indisputable evidence of human occupation at Fell's Cave in Patagonia, near the southern tip of South America, is dated to 9000–8000 B.C. In fact, though, it has been calculated that human beings could easily have traveled the 10,000 miles between the coast of Alaska to the tip of South America in 1,000 years: That would mean only 10 miles a year. Still, this was an amazing phenomenon in human history—the peopling of two complete continents in a relatively short period of time.

The question then becomes, Why? What motivated these people to keep moving into unknown territories? Were they all imbued with the spirit of explorers? Hardly likely. More likely is that they were simply seeking more congenial climates and environments. Drought conditions may often have played a role. More particularly, they were driven to seek food, for that was apparently the major if not their sole concern and occupation. These people subsisted almost entirely on hunting and food gathering. The former included birds and

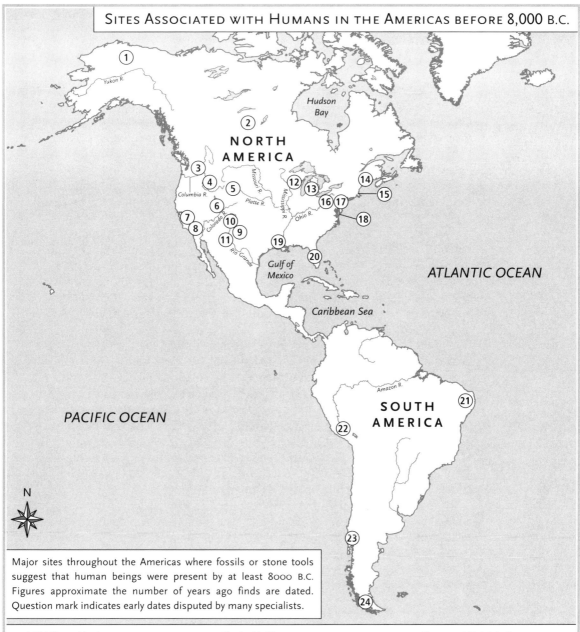

SITES ASSOCIATED WITH HUMANS IN THE AMERICAS BEFORE 8,000 B.C.

NORTH AMERICA

Yukon R.

Hudson Bay

Columbia R.

Missouri R.

Platte R.

Mississippi R.

Ohio R.

Colorado R.

Rio Grande

Gulf of Mexico

ATLANTIC OCEAN

Caribbean Sea

PACIFIC OCEAN

Amazon R.

SOUTH AMERICA

N

Major sites throughout the Americas where fossils or stone tools suggest that human beings were present by at least 8000 B.C. Figures approximate the number of years ago finds are dated. Question mark indicates early dates disputed by many specialists.

1. ?Old Crow, Alaska 30,000
2. ?Taber, Alberta, Canada 24,000
3. Snake River, Wash. 10,000
4. Wilson Butte, Idaho 11,000
5. Colby, Wyo. 11,000
6. Danger Cave, Utah 10,000
7. ?Calico, Calif. 200,000
8. ?San Diego, Calif. 40,000

9. Clovis, N. Mex. 12,000
10. Folsom, N. Mex. 10,000
11. ?Orogrande, N. Mex. 30,000
12. Big Eddy Falls, Wisc. 11,000
13. Gainey, Mich. 11,000
14. Vail, Maine 11,000
15. Nantucket, Mass. 10,000
16. ?Meadowcroft, Pa. 17,500

17. Shawnee-Minisink, Pa. 11,000
18. Tilghman, Md. 10,000
19. John Pearce, La. 10,000
20. Little Salt Spring, Fla. 11,000
21. ?Pedra Furada, Brazil 48,000
22. ?Pikimachay, Peru 20,000
23. ?Monte Verde, Chile 13,000
24. ?Fell's Cave, Argentina 11,000

The First Watercraft

Until it was established that human beings were present in Australia as early as 50,000 B.C., it was not necessary to consider that watercraft had been invented anywhere near that early. The islands where humans had appeared earlier than that were at the time of settlement linked by land (due to lower sea level), so humans could have walked or at least waded across. For example, Japan was joined to Siberia and Korea, Sri Lanka was joined to India, the Philippines were joined to the East Indies and so to the mainland. But the case of Australia has forced students of that era to imagine what kind of watercraft these very early "sailors" had.

The oldest known boats to survive are some from ancient Egyptian tombs dated to about 2500 B.C., and these have survived only because the Egyptians themselves placed them in such dry environments that they did not rot away. Long before the sophisticated boats of the Egyptians, though, there had to have been all kinds of primitive watercraft, for it is evident from the evidence of human presence at several locations that at least some early humans did get around on the water.

Undoubtedly the first watercraft were simply rafts made of plant materials. Even the most primitive people would have observed that quite large branches floated. From that, it would have been an easy step to realize that if a large log could float, that log could be hollowed out to hold a person who could then control the direction of the craft. Rafts and dugout canoes, then, must have sufficed to provide water transport for many thousands of years. Canoes made of bark may also have appeared very early. But because all these watercraft were made of vegetable matter, and especially because they got wet, they rotted away quite quickly without leaving a trace behind. The oldest known dugout, for instance, was found in Holland and is dated to only 6300 B.C.

At some point, people in various parts of the world would have begun to devise variations on these two basic craft. Depending on the plant forms in their region, they would have made rafts of reed, for example, and once they began to tie bundles of reeds together, they probably realized they could make a more seaworthy craft if they shaped the reeds somewhat—build up the sides or a prow, for instance, to keep much of the water out. Likewise, canoemakers would

marine species as well as large land animals. The latter included nuts, fruits, berries, roots, and any plants they identified as edible. And probably the Paleo-Indians found that the prey and the "picking" were easier to come by if they just kept moving into virgin territory. It may also have been that in the competition for food, some of these people crowded out others, and that, too, contributed to the rapid dispersal.

The lifestyles and tools of the Clovis and Folsom hunter-gatherers of North America were in many ways similar to those of other

have found some trees made lighter and more manageable boats. Meanwhile, some people realized they could sew skins together and stretch them around a light wooden frame to form a type of boat known as a coracle. Others probably realized they could inflate the skins of animals and use them to make rafts.

Such craft were probably the only ones known by human beings for thousands of years. Other refinements would have come much later. Some ancient people discovered that hollow clay pots served to support a raft; others found that even large clay "tubs" would float. The Polynesians constructed outriggers, whereas American Indians made their canoes from birch bark.

Reed—stalks of a type of thick grass—was used by some of the first people to make watercraft. This boat, used to this day by sailors in parts of India, is undoubtedly more elaborate than the first reed boats, but it utilizes the same material. (© Philip Baird www.anthroarcheart.org)

peoples of this period throughout the then-inhabited world. Most people still hunted wild nomadic herd animals and ranged widely in search of food sources. It should be understood, too, that as widespread as human beings had become by about 8000 B.C., the world was still quite sparsely inhabited. In most instances, there were still relatively small bands of people roaming relatively small areas—not much more than extended families in many cases, or perhaps loosely formed bands of up to 50 adults.

A CHANGING WORLD

About 8000 B.C., major changes began to occur throughout much of the inhabited world. The world's climate was warming relatively rapidly, the great ice caps and glaciers had by then melted, new plant and animal species were taking over the territory formerly dominated by the large animals. Whether because of this climate change or other causes such as the spread of disease pathogens and overhunting by humans, many of the large animals throughout the world began to become extinct. In particular, those hunted by the

The bison pictured here was painted on the cave of Lascaux, in southwest central France, about 15,000 B.C. These large, wild animals were hunted down in such numbers by the people of that period that they eventually became extinct in Europe, just as many large, wild animals in the Americas would also become extinct. *(Larry Dale Gordon/Getty Images)*

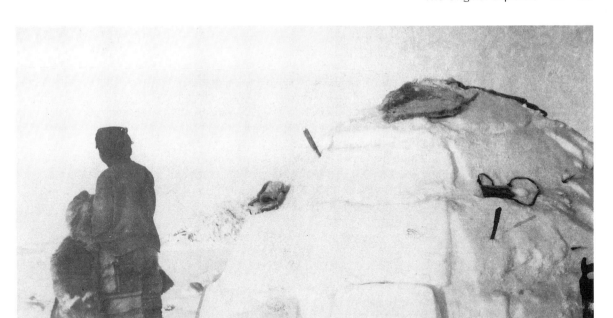

Anthropologists believe that the first wave of humans—Paleo-Eskimos—may have arrived on Greenland as early as 2500 B.C., in which case they very likely were already making igloos like the one pictured here on Baffin Island in the 1920s. *(Library of Congress, Prints and Photographs Division [LC-USZ62-103524])*

Paleo-Indians in the Americas all became extinct, while in Europe and Asia, such animals as the woolly mammoths, rhinoceroses, cave bears, cave lions, Irish elk, large bison, and other giant species also became extinct. (Pygmy mammoths survived to as late as 4000 B.C. on an island in Siberia.) The extinctions in Africa did not proceed as rapidly, and some giant fauna still survive there—elephants, rhinoceros, giraffe, hippo, and gorillas. This may account in part for why sub-Saharan Africans at least did not feel the need to participate in the next major step in the development of human history—what is known as the Neolithic Revolution.

Neolithic literally means "new stone" and is the term used to distinguish a major period in the development of human culture. As with all such phases, the Neolithic Age did not begin at the same time and in the same way everywhere in the world, but in general it was underway about 8000 B.C. By singling out stone, the term emphasizes that this period saw the development of a much more elaborate stone "toolkit." But the reason there were more tools and more specialized tools was that there were more specialized tasks to be accomplished. Indeed, many of the tools were made from bone and antlers and eventually some began to be made from metal such as copper. They began to make objects out of fibers—both baskets and textiles—and clay. They also began to domesticate animals such as sheep and cattle.

Perhaps the most significant development, however, was that peoples in many parts of the world began to cultivate plants of various

Discovering the Pacific Islands

One area of the world often overlooked in histories of discovery and exploration is Oceania, the name for the main islands in the Pacific Ocean. In part this may be because it is so hard to reconstruct a history that all the experts agree on: It is not so much that they disagree as the simple fact that there is so little solid evidence to rely on. Modern students have divided the islands into three groups: the Melanesians, Micronesians, and Polynesians. (*-Nesians* is a Greek suffix meaning "islands," *mela-* means "black," *micro-* means "small," and *poly-* means "many.") These groupings refer to certain physical and cultural aspects of the native peoples, but they should not be taken as some absolute categories.

The major islands of the Melanesians include New Guinea, Bismarck Archipelago, the Solomons, New Hebrides, New Caledonia, and Fiji. New Guinea and perhaps several others were settled as far back as 40,000 years ago; starting about 1600 B.C., a new wave of settlers apparently began to come over from Southeast Asia—Indonesia or the Philippines. The Micronesians include the Marianas, Marshalls, Carolines, Gilberts, Wake, and Guam islands. It is possible that one or more were settled as early as 4000 B.C. by people from the Philippines and Indonesia, but most were not settled until after 1600 B.C., whether from Melanesian islands to their west or more waves from Southeast Asia.

Then there are the Polynesian islands, which include Hawaii, Midway, Tonga, Marquesas, Samoas, Society, Cook, Tahiti, and New Zealand. Tonga may have been settled by 1200 B.C., but most of the rest—with two major exceptions—were not settled until between 500 and 300 B.C. Those exceptions are the two of the best known groups of the Polynesians—Hawaii Islands and New Zealand. The Hawaii Islands were not settled until about A.D. 300–500. New Zealand was not settled until sometime between A.D. 750 and 1000.

Some of these islands may have been connected by land bridges, but most required people to make their way by boats. This required skills both in boat-making and navigation, and the first to reach these islands deserve to be known as among the first anonymous explorers.

kinds—that is, turn to agriculture. This, along with the activities referred to above, meant that people were settling down in more permanent and ambitious settlements. As these settlements produced more reliable food supplies and other aids to survival, populations began to grow. The Neolithic Revolution, in other words, marked the beginning of village life and larger populations, which in turn would lead to the growth of cities.

By 3000 B.C., then, the world had greatly changed. Settlements, although still relatively scattered, now existed across much of the world. In addition to the lands already identified as inhabited, people had moved into still more locales. The island of Crete, for example, was settled by at least 6500 B.C. The first wave of Paleo-Eskimos had moved into Alaska from Siberia by at least 3000 B.C., for it was about then that the first wave began to move across Arctic North America. Indeed, by 3000 B.C., it is easier to list the places on the earth where no human beings had yet set foot. Antarctica, of course, was not only an untouched but an unknown continent. Many parts of the Arctic region also remained unexplored—the Paleo-Eskimos probably did not get to Greenland until about 2500 B.C. The many islands of the Pacific beyond the Philippines and New Guinea—including New Zealand—were still uninhabited and probably still unknown, as were a few islands off Africa's northwest coast: the Azores, the Canaries, the Madeiras. Madagascar, the large island only some 250 miles off Africa's southeast coast, may have been known but it was not yet inhabited. Then, too, large regions of the continental landmasses were untouched—the Himalayan region, for instance, or the Rocky Mountains, the highest Andes, the largest deserts.

Still, by 3000 B.C., before any individuals recognized today as "explorers" even set out, most of the world had been discovered. Not inhabited, not even thoroughly explored, nevertheless human beings had exerted themselves, crossed bodies of water, climbed mountains, endured extreme cold and heat, and confronted fierce animals to move into unknown territory. Once again the question arises, What motivated people to move into so many distant, even inhospitable regions? And as will be seen, even settling into large and comfortable cities does not destroy that desire. And along with the civilization that is almost defined by city life, there emerges the ability to write and record. With this skill, human beings embark on a new phase of discovery and exploration.

3

EARLY ANCIENT EXPLORERS

 The first societies that were based in cities and that would have the most influence on later Western history were those that emerged in the Near East and the eastern Mediterranean. Radiating out from their urban centers, these peoples ranged ever farther into unknown lands and seas. These early expeditions and explorers were not motivated by some selfless desire to shed light on the unknown. Rather, most were engaged in trade or diplomacy or conquest. Whatever their motives, because these civilizations simultaneously developed systems of writing, some of their members are credited today with being among the earliest of explorers.

THE EARLY MESOPOTAMIANS

The first major societies based on city-states, at least as measured by their influence on later Western civilization, were the ones that emerged in the region between the Tigris and Euphrates rivers about 4000 B.C. This region is generally known as Mesopotamia—"between the rivers"—and for at least the next 3,500 years it was the homeland for a series of different dominating peoples. The first of these were the Sumerians, a people of unknown origins who appeared in southern Mesopotamia and soon were developing a number of small but powerful city-states: Eridu, Kish, Lagash, Nippur, Umma, Ur, and Uruk. The Sumerians were an inventive people—they appear to have been the first to develop a coherent system of writing and among the first to use wheeled vehicles—and they were also active traders. In search of prized metals, stone, and wood, some of them went into the distant mountains of Armenia, the Taurus Mountains of Turkey, over into Central Asia and Afghanistan, and even down into northern India. Others sailed out along the Persian Gulf, apparently even as far south as the mouth of the Indus River in northwestern India and possibly west around the Arabian Peninsula as far as the Red Sea.

The script that the Sumerians developed is known as cuneiform—"wedge-form." A sharp stylus was used to cut the letters into damp clay, leaving small impressions that were pointed at the interior and wider at the surface (like a wedge). The clay was then baked to

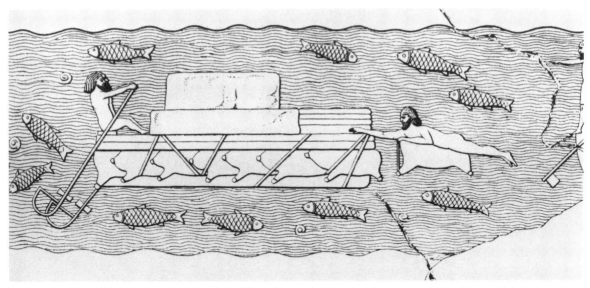

The vessel depicted in a stone carving from the Palace of Sennacherib in present-day Iraq and dated to about 700 B.C. is transporting goods on the Tigris River in Mesopotamia. It is essentially a raft of inflated animal skins—and note the man floating on a similar inflated skin being pulled along behind. *(From* Ninive et l'Assyrie, *Vol. III, by V. Place. Paris, 1867)*

retain the writing, and since the clay tablets have survived, there are records of many of the Sumerians' varied activities. The names of the individuals who made specific journeys, however, were not recorded. Then, about 2350 B.C., a man from the relatively obscure city of Akkad, or Agade (probably in what is now southern Iraq, but no remains have yet been found), set about to conquer most of these Sumerian city-states. He soon controlled not only all of southern Mesopotamia but also much of the region to his east (modern Iran) and to his west (Syria, Palestine, and Turkey). As Sargon of Akkad, he is said to have ruled for 61 years, in effect the first great emperor in history.

Various poems and inscriptions from Mesopotamia of this era refer to distant lands, most of which cannot be identified with complete certainty, but it is clear that the Sumerians were at least aware of the sources of many products from Africa to Turkey. But it is Sargon of Akkad himself who allegedly left an account of a naval expedition that he led "across the sea in the west" and conquered Anaku-ki, Kapptara-ki, "and lands beyond the upper sea." Scholars debate just what these places were, some claiming he went as far as Spain, others saying he was referring to Cyprus and Crete, while still others say he never got beyond the Persian Gulf.

The dynasty founded by Sargon of Akkad ended within 200 years, and for the next 1,500 years a succession of other rulers dominated Mesopotamia, most of them based in the city of Babylon. As powerful and imperial as some of these rulers were, the Mesopotamians did not seem especially interested in setting sail for destinations unknown. They do not seem to have ventured far beyond the Persian Gulf or the eastern coast of the Mediterranean. They do not seem to have used sails on their boats until long after other maritime peoples had adopted them. They were, in fact, a relatively self-contained people, with a way-of-life focused on their rivers.

THE EGYPTIANS

More or less parallel to the Mesopotamian world, both in time and space, another great river-based civilization was thriving—ancient Egypt. It emerged into recorded history about 3200 B.C., and this is embodied in a beautiful carved stone tablet depicting Narmer, the first king of a united Egypt. Some scholars interpret other carvings on the stone to indicate that Narmer may have even gone into Mesopotamia. During the next 300 years, successors to Narmer appear to have sent trade or military missions into the Sinai Peninsula and up as far as the Black Sea.

Egyptians and Ships

The Egyptians can not be credited with inventing ships: Various people all over the world independently invented watercraft of all kinds. It so happens, though, that no other people left so much physical evidence of watercraft as they evolved across the centuries. Carvings, wall paintings, vase designs, textile designs, models—the ancient Egyptians left a wonderful record that probably reflects the evolution of watercraft among many ancient peoples.

Their earliest craft, like those of so many peoples, were probably only rafts made of reeds, and none of these have survived. But by at least 3500 B.C., they were shaping the reed into long, narrow boats: Numerous drawings exist that depict these early vessels, some with high prows and sterns, some with cabin-like structures, most with multiple oars. Then an Egyptian vase painting dated to about 3100 B.C. depicts a small sail on a boat—one of the earliest if not the earliest depiction of a sailboat.

Egyptian boats for the next few centuries continued to be made of reed and probably seldom ventured beyond the Nile River. By about 2700 B.C., however, the Egyptians were using wood at least to reinforce some parts of their reed boats—providing platforms to stand on, for instance. Most likely they very quickly began to make all wood boats. The Egyptians built them with planks of wood with no internal ribs or keel, and this basic form of construction at first produced flat-bottom, square-ended boats that were not much more than barges. And by about 1800 B.C., the Egyptians were building rivercraft more than 200 feet long and 70 feet wide to haul the heavy stone required for their monumental temples and other structures.

The Egyptians' method of constructing boats—that is, building up a shell of planks rather than starting with a "skeleton" of a keel and frame—was used throughout much of the world for many centuries to come. But it does not seem to have limited the ancient Egyptians when it came to building the sleeker ships designed for open seas. As early as 2450 B.C., Egyptians were building quite

For the most part, though, the lives of Egyptians were centered on the Nile River, and reed boats of all sizes moved up and down the river carrying produce and materials. Once the Egyptians began to make wooden boats, they recognized all too well that their land did not have enough trees. An inscribed stone (now in Palermo, Italy) describes how about 2700 B.C. Egyptian Pharaoh Sneferu "brought 40 ships of cedar-wood" from Byblos, a Phoenician port city on the Mediterranean. Sneferu is also said to have led a military expedition into the land south of Egypt known as Nubia, and some 250 years later, an Egyptian named Harkhuf reported that he had been sent to Nubia "to explore a road to this country. I did so in only seven months and I brought back gifts of all kinds . . . 300 asses loaded with incense, ebony, grain, panthers, ivory, and every good

trim wooden ships for sailing on ocean water, and the seagoing ships depicted in the reliefs at Queen Hatshepsut's burial temple are estimated to be some 90 feet long. Egyptian seagoing ships had two features not required by river craft: a rope truss that connected the bow and the stern and could be adjusted like a tourniquet to keep the front and end of the boat from sagging; and a rope netting that encircled the upper part of the hull to keep the planks from separating under pressure from the deck and cargo.

Many of the Egyptians' rivercraft depended on humanpower—rowing, paddling, poling—but sails were also used on many boats, either alone or with humanpower. At first the masts were simple poles, but as the boats became larger and required heavier sails, the Egyptians turned to "two-legged" masts: poles tilted from each side of the boat to join at their top ends. By 2200 B.C., however, the Egyptians had found a way to make single pole masts to support even the heaviest sails required for seagoing ships.

Because sails were made of easily perishable material, it is not known exactly when they were first used, but this is the oldest known picture of a ship with a sail. It is from an ancient Egyptian vase dated to about 3200 B.C. (From Studies in Early Pottery of the Near East, Vol. 1, by Henri Frankfort. London: Royal Anthropological Institute of Great Britain and Ireland, 1924)

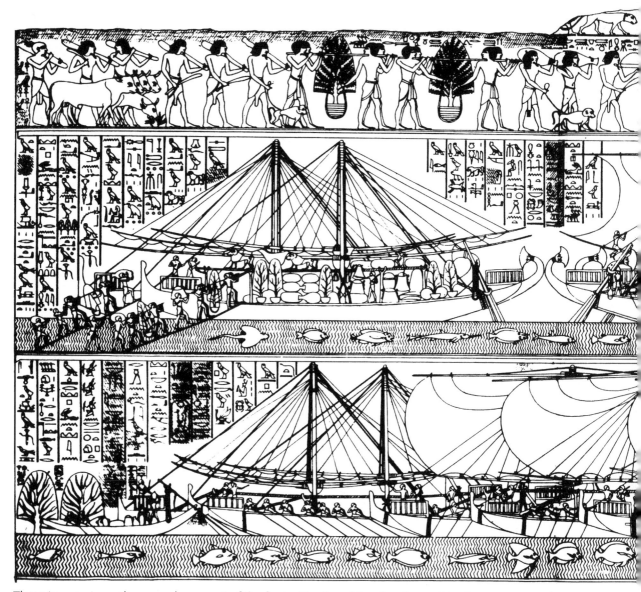

These impressive sailing vessels are part of the fleet of trading ships that Queen Hatshepsut sent to the "land of Punt" (possibly Somaliland, possibly India) about 1492 B.C. Carved on the Temple of Deir el-Bahri along the Nile, where Hatshepsut was buried, they provide a remarkable image of the advanced nature of maritime trade by that time. *(From* Deir-el-Bahari, *by Auguste Mariette, Leipzig, 1877)*

product." (He also said he brought back a "dancing dwarf" as a present to the king—possibly an African pygmy, a member of one of the peoples in equatorial Africa—such as the Mbute or Batwa—who are particularly small.) Nubia, which extended from the bor-

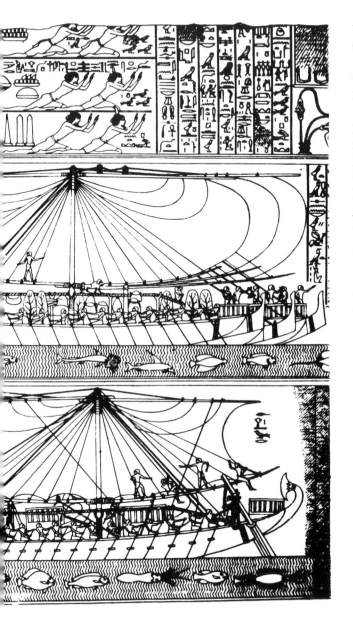

their control, although they had commercial dealings with black Africans.

Several Egyptian pharaohs, however, did conduct military campaigns that took them into Mesopotamia, Syria, ancient Phoenicia (Lebanon), and Asia Minor (Turkey). The most notable expedition, however, was not a military campaign but a combination diplomatic and commercial mission sponsored by Queen Hatshepsut, who effectively ruled Egypt between about 1505 and 1485 B.C. About 1492 B.C. she sent Egyptian ships under the command of Nehsi down the Red Sea and into the Indian Ocean to what was called the Land of Punt, which some scholars believe referred to Somaliland, on the horn of Africa, while others believe it referred to India. This was not the first time Egyptians had visited the Land of Punt, but it was not until Hatshepsut's expedition that regular trade was maintained between the two lands. The famous carved reliefs at the great temple of Deir el-Bahri along the Nile, where Queen Hatshepsut was buried, depict the magnificent sailing ships that the Egyptians possessed by this time.

Under Thutmose III, who ruled for some 30 years after Hatshepsut's death, Egypt attained its most expansive empire, controlling the entire eastern Mediterranean coast and up into the northern reaches of the Tigris and Euphrates rivers and extended Egypt's southern borders down into Sudan and along the coast of the Red Sea. One of the aides to Thutmose III described how the pharaoh, after crossing the Euphrates River, moved into Syria and "hunted 120 elephants for the sake of their tusks."

During this time, too, Egypt traded with peoples as far removed as Crete and Greece and possibly even Malta, but there is reason to believe that the Egyptians left much of the long-haul trade to others: That is, the Egyptians preferred to import and export wares by

der of southern Egypt (roughly, Aswan on the Nile) into northern Sudan, was about as far south as the ancient Egyptians ever imposed

staying put in their own ports and letting for-
eigners do the sailing. The Egyptians, in fact,
were not that interested in exploring beyond
their circle of familiar trading partners.

MINOANS AND MYCENAEANS

One people who did range widely across the
Mediterranean Sea during this era were the
Minoans, who between 2500 and 1500 B.C.
conducted a bustling commercial empire
based on the island of Crete. Perhaps because
their homeland was so relatively small—
almost exactly the area of Puerto Rico—the
people of Crete had always looked outward
both to import needed products and to export
their own wares. Even before the emergence of
the Minoan civilization—so named by modern
archaeologists after a mythical Cretan king,

Minos—Cretans were trading with Egypt;
Minoans also traded with the island of Cyprus
and other islands throughout the Aegean.
There is some evidence to suggest that
Minoans also sailed as far west as Italy and
even Spain. In the east, Minoans seem to have
had at least trade contacts with Turkey,
Afghanistan, and India.

About 1500 B.C., Greeks from the mainland
appear to have moved over to Crete and taken
over from the Minoans. Usually referred to as
Mycenaeans, after their main city on the
mainland, these Greeks also took over many
of the Minoans' overseas commercial routes
and contacts. But the Mycenaeans were
apparently not all that interested in seeking
out new lands or dominating foreign trade,
and this left the field open to some of the most
enterprising and adventurous people of the
ancient world, the Phoenicians.

This Minoan sailboat is accompanied by dolphins
as it makes its way across the Mediterranean about
1300 B.C. Note the high prow, designed to cut
through the waves. It is carved on a sealstone, a
piece of stone about the size of a five-cent piece
that was pressed into clay to identify the owner.
(From The Palace Minos, Vol. 1, by Arthur Evans. London: Macmillan and Co., 1921)

THE PHOENICIANS

The Phoenicians were a people who lived
largely along the coasts of what are modern
Syria, Lebanon, and Israel. Their name comes
for the Greek word *phoinix*, meaning "red-
purple," in recognition of the fact that these
people were famous for trading in reddish
purple dyed goods, primarily textiles. Sometimes known as Canaanites from Old Testament references, the Phoenicians identified
themselves usually as Sidonians, after Sidon,
one of their major cities, because they never
organized into one nation state. But if the
Phoenicians were backward when it came to
institutional organization, they were among
the most progressive of ancient peoples when
it came to artful crafts, manufacturing, trade,
and colonization. They also developed an
alphabet that the Greeks and Romans bor-
rowed and from which all Western alphabets
have since been developed.

Considering that the Phoenicians had an alphabet and kept such careful records, it might seem strange that they did not leave accounts of their far-ranging voyages. The evidence, instead, comes from other peoples' accounts and from the physical remains that the Phoenicians left in many distant locales. The earliest recorded record of Phoenicians as traders was the Egyptian account of the Pharaoh Sneferu's expedition to import cedar wood from Byblos, one of the major Phoenician port cities. Cedar and other trees, plentiful in the Lebanon range that backed the coastal cities of the Phoenicians, would remain one of their major exports.

As early as 1200 B.C., with the decline of the Minoans and the lack of interest by the Egyptians, the Phoenicians were already prominent if not dominant mariners in the eastern Mediterranean. Greek traditions claimed that the Phoenicians were soon thereafter founding colonies in the western Mediterranean—Utica in Tunisia, Gades (Cadiz) in Spain, Nora in Sardinia. Modern

This carving from the Palace of Sargon at Khorsabad (modern Iraq) is dated to about 715 B.C. It depicts three Phoenician cargo vessels loading and towing logs—most likely cedar from Lebanon, a major export product of the Phoenicians who lived along the east coast of the Mediterranean. *(Library of Congress, Prints and Photographs Division [LC-USZ6-929])*

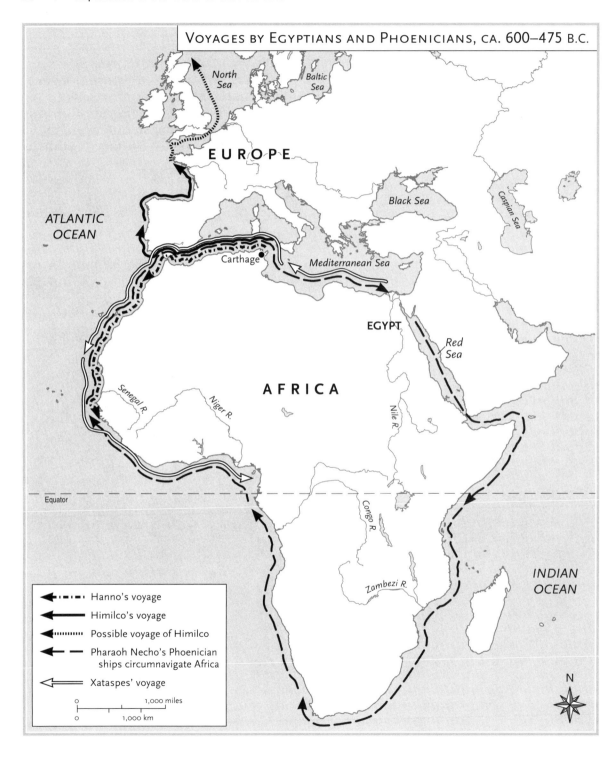

VOYAGES BY EGYPTIANS AND PHOENICIANS, CA. 600–475 B.C.

North
Sea

Baltic
Sea

EUROPE

ATLANTIC
OCEAN

Black Sea

Caspian Sea

Carthage

Mediterranean Sea

EGYPT

Red
Sea

Senegal R.

Niger R.

AFRICA

Nile R.

Equator

Congo R.

Zambezi R.

INDIAN
OCEAN

⬅•—•— Hanno's voyage

⬅——— Himilco's voyage

⬅•••••••• Possible voyage of Himilco

⬅— — Pharaoh Necho's Phoenician
ships circumnavigate Africa

⬅═══ Xataspes' voyage

0   1,000 miles

0   1,000 km

N

archaeologists do not confirm such early dates but they do agree that Phoenicians were definitely establishing colonies in those very sites by about 700 B.C. The most famous of their colonies was that of Carthage, founded by Phoenicians on the coast of Tunisia about 800 B.C. Carthage soon became a major trading center in the western Mediterranean and began to establish its own colonies all around the coast of Spain and on the Balearic Islands, on Sicily and Malta, and on Corsica and Sardinia. Although at first they do not seem to have resorted to force, the Carthaginians seemed determined to beat out their Greek rivals in the western Mediterranean and by about 500 B.C. they had colonies on the North African coast opposite Gibraltar and so controlled traffic through the Strait of Gibraltar—the Pillars of Hercules to the Greeks.

Once they were solidly established at the far end of the Mediterranean, the Carthaginians evidently decided to venture out into the Atlantic. There are two major expeditions by Carthaginians; ironically, both are known about solely from texts by the Phoenicians' enemies, ancient Greeks and Romans. One of these was a voyage by Himilco, who about 500 B.C., according to the first century A.D. Roman historian Pliny the Elder, passed into the North Atlantic as far as the French coast of Brittany. Some modern scholars claim Himilco went as far as Cornwall, the southwestern tip of Britain, reached some 200 years later by Pytheas; others claim he went out into the North Atlantic as far as the Sargasso Sea, well past the Azores. Such extreme claims are rejected by most scholars, and everything about Himilco's voyage remains questionable.

A somewhat more solid story is that involving the expedition of a contemporary of Himilco and a fellow Carthaginian, Hanno. He was said to have posted an account of his voyage at a temple in Carthage when he returned, and it is that account that is quoted by Polybius, a Greek historian of the second century B.C.:

> He set sail with sixty vessels of fifty oars and a multitude of men and women to the number of 30,000 and provisions and other equipment. After putting out to sea and passing the Pillars [of Hercules] we sailed beyond them for two days.

At this point, Hanno, unlike Himilco, turned south and proceeded down the northwest coast of Africa:

> We sailed on for half a day until we arrived at a lagoon full of high and thick-grown cane. This was haunted by elephants and multitudes of other grazing beasts.

Continuing down along the coast, Hanno went ashore at various points and reported all manner of exotic sights:

> Beyond these dwelt inhospitable Ethiopians [Africans]. Their land is infested with wild beasts. . . . These highlands are inhabited by a freakish race of men, the Troglodytes [from Greek for "hole dwellers," here referring to some unknown African people] who are said to run faster than horses. . . . Sailing on from that point we came to another deep and wide river, which was infested with crocodiles and hippopotami. . . . The second island was full of wild people. By far the greater number were women with hairy bodies. Our interpreters called them Gorillas.

There are numerous problems raised by Hanno's voyage, but the major one is just how

Fictitious Explorations

Separating fact from fiction is difficult when it comes to knowing exactly how much of the world was explored by the ancients. In part this is because they often lacked the means to observe, to measure, and to record "facts" about their world; information was passed on largely by word of mouth, and this inevitably led to errors and distortions. Beyond that, ancient peoples placed great faith in myths and legends and were not necessarily anxious to displace these with "scientific" evidence. It is no wonder, then, that some of the earliest stories about discovery and exploration involve what people today regard as fictional accounts.

Perhaps the most famous of the poems of the Babylonians, for instance, recounted the story of Gilgamesh. He was said to have been a powerful and oppressive ruler who, after conquering several city-states in southern Mesopotamia, traveled down into southern Arabian peninsula, crossed the Arabian Sea and went over to the island of Socotra off Somaliland and possibly even on to Somaliland itself. Although the best surviving copy of this epic dates to only the seventh century B.C., it is known to include myths, folklore, and tales dating back to well before 2000 B.C. Although clearly fictional, the poem served to introduce the Babylonians to a world beyond their narrow confines.

The Egyptians, meanwhile, had their own story of a merchant who claimed to have been sent by a pharaoh on a business trip; when his ship was wrecked in a storm, he alone survived and was washed up on an island. The island was rich in fruits and animal life, and after an encounter with a giant snake, the merchant was rescued by a ship that the snake had loaded with fine products to bring back to Egypt. The story was written down on a papyrus as early as 2000 B.C. and seems to be describing a journey to the Land of Punt, variously located in India, Africa, or Arabia.

Scholars have noted certain elements in these two famous tales that recur in later works, including the Old Testament of the Bible and Homer's *Odyssey*. This may have been due to a direct influence of these works, but it may also represent simply the recurrence of certain themes in the ancient world. And although these stories cannot be used as true geography or history texts, they probably reflect some knowledge of the world of that era.

far down the coast of Africa he went. Some scholars say he got no farther than Morocco, on the northwestern shoulder; at the other extreme, some scholars say he got all the way to Sierra Leone, only 8 degrees above the equator. If the latter, Hanno was some 3,000 miles from Carthage, making for a round-trip almost as ambitious as that of Columbus's, and it would be 2,000 years before any European got as far down the coast of Africa.

The Phoenicians are credited with voyages in many other directions and regions. By 650

B.C. they were a prominent presence in the Indian Ocean; some modern scholars have claimed they got to the East Indies—even to China—but such claims find no support among most serious scholars. Then there are those who insist that some Phoenicians reached the Americas, whether by accidentally being driven there by winds or by deliberately seeking new lands. The supporters of this theory cite various inscriptions they claim to be the Phoenician language, as well as other finds such as coins, but most serious scholars reject all such claims.

One story of a major Phoenician expedition, however, has been the subject of serious debate almost since the time it was first reported. That is the voyage sponsored by the Egyptian pharaoh Necho about 600 B.C. Once again, the only source for this story is the ancient Greek historian Herodotus, and he devotes only one brief paragraph to it:

> Africa is clearly surrounded by water except where it touches Asia. Necho, pharaoh of Egypt, was the first person we know of to demonstrate this. After he had finished digging out a canal between the Nile and the Red Sea, he sent out a naval expedition manned by Phoenicians, instructing them to come back by entering the Mediterranean through the Pillars of Hercules and in that way return to Egypt. Setting out from the Red Sea, the Phoenicians sailed into the Indian Ocean. Each autumn they put in at whatever part of Africa they happened to be sailing by; there they planted crops and stayed until harvest time, reaped the grain, and then sailed on. In that way, two years passed and it was not until the third year that they entered the Pillars of Hercules and made their way back to Egypt. They reported many things that others can believe if they choose to, but I cannot—in particular, that while sailing around Africa they had the sun on their right side.

Most scholars just find it hard to accept such a feat at such an early point in history. It could be done, they agree—scholars have calculated the way these sailors could have had favorable weather, then put ashore for several months required to grow a crop of grain. Scholars also point out that the very detail Herodotus singles out as disproving such a story actually supports it: Namely, if the sailors had rounded the tip of Africa, the sun would often have been to the north—that is, to their right.

In the end, the Phoenicians, for all their initiative and ambition when it came to sailing, colonizing, and trading, showed little interest in exploring for the sake of discovering the unknown or of adding to the sum of their contemporaries' knowledge.

THE PERSIANS

About the time the Phoenicians' reputation as master mariners was at its peak, with their commercial empire extending from the shores of the eastern Mediterranean to the Pillars of Hercules, a new power had emerged in the Near East—the Persians. Their homeland was modern Iran and Afghanistan, and by 549 B.C. Cyrus the Great had expanded the Persians' power through conquest so that they controlled territory from the Mediterranean coast all the way to what is now Pakistan. In fact, the Persians controlled the Phoenicians' own homeland as well as Mesopotamia, and Cyrus's successors would extend Persian power still farther—including parts of northern Greece, Egypt, and Libya.

The Persians ruled this vast empire with a relatively light hand, allowing most peoples to continue in their own ways—retaining

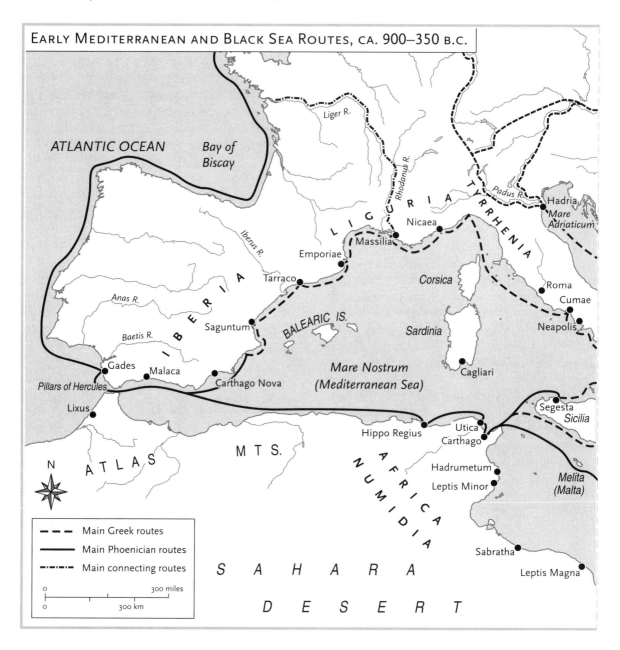

EARLY MEDITERRANEAN AND BLACK SEA ROUTES, CA. 900–350 B.C.

ATLANTIC OCEAN

Bay of Biscay

Liger R.

Rhodanus R.

LIGURIA

TYRRHENIA

Padus R.

Hadria

Mare Adriaticum

Nicaea

Massilia

Emporiae

Iberus R.

Tarraco

Corsica

Roma

Cumae

Anas R.

IBERIA

Saguntum

BALEARIC IS.

Sardinia

Neapolis

Baetis R.

Gades

Malaca

Carthago Nova

Mare Nostrum (Mediterranean Sea)

Cagliari

Pillars of Hercules

Lixus

Hippo Regius

Utica

Carthago

Segesta

Sicilia

N

ATLAS   MTS.

AFRICA

NUMIDIA

Hadrumetum

Leptis Minor

Melita (Malta)

--- Main Greek routes
— Main Phoenician routes
—·— Main connecting routes

0   300 miles
0   300 km

S A H A R A

D E S E R T

Sabratha

Leptis Magna

their languages, religions, cultures. The Persians were more interested in trade and taxes, and to advance this they encouraged caravans to cross their land, exchanging wares between Europe and Asia. That is why they allowed the Greeks and Phoenicians living along the eastern Mediterranean coast to continue their own activities. The Persians

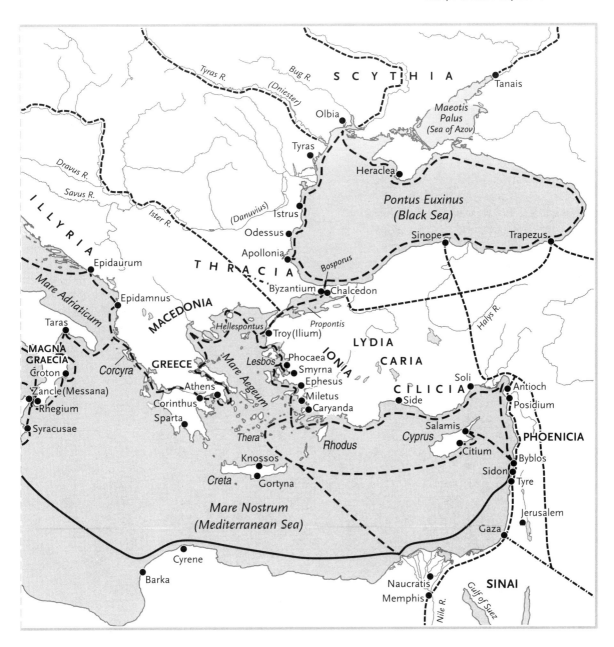

also built a network of roads connecting the major cities of their empire. Although their ships sailed all around the Persian Gulf and the Arabian Sea, they were essentially a land-based empire that looked more to the east than to the west.

Unfortunately, almost none of the Persians' own accounts of their discoveries survive because Alexander the Great, when he conquered the Persians, destroyed most of their records. However, Herodotus, a Greek historian, described an important expedition sponsored by the Persian emperor Darius, who ruled 586–521 B.C.

> The greater part of Asia was explored by Darius, who desired to know more about the Indus River, which is one of the two rivers in the world to produce crocodiles. He wanted to know where this river runs out onto the sea and sent in ships both those on whom he could rely to make a true report and also Scylax of Caryanda.
>
> They set out from the city of Caspatyrus in the land of Pactyike, sailed down the river toward the east and to the sea. Sailing westward over the sea, they came in the thirtieth month to the place from where the king of the Egyptians had sent out the Phoenicians of whom I have spoken earlier [the expedition of Necho] to sail around Africa.

There are many problems with this text, but some scholars believe that Pactyike was in eastern Afghanistan and that Caspatyrus was somewhere along the Kabul River, which took Scylax to the Indus. Once in the Arabian Sea, Scylax evidently sailed across the Indian Ocean, up into the Persian Gulf, then down and around the Arabian Peninsula, and up into the Red Sea all the way to the Egyptian port of Suez.

Aside from problems with the geographic details of this voyage, what is interesting is that Scylax himself was a Greek. His home city, Caryanda, was in Caria, over on the south-

By 400 B.C., a growing number of sailors, merchants, travelers, and writers from the Mesopotamian and Mediterranean world were beginning to have firsthand experience with the Indian Ocean, and they would have been familiar with boats like these sailing along the northwestern coast of India. *(Library of Congress, Prints and Photographs Division [LC-D4271-384])*

western Mediterranean coast of Turkey, and then under Persian rule. His role in this expedition thus confirms the sense that the Persians were open to people of "foreign" extraction.

Scylax, by the way, was so respected in his day that a periplus, or sailing guide, was attributed to him, even though it clearly was composed at least two centuries later—about 350 B.C. Known as the *Periplus of Scylax*, it was an amazingly detailed guide to the many islands, rivers, harbors, towns, and even peoples bordering the Mediterranean and Black Seas and the waters connecting them, even providing the distances between all the identified places. In fact, it is so thorough that many scholars believe that what has survived to this day is a work that was heavily revised and reworked in later centuries.

There was another famous Persian exploratory expedition, this one involving a cousin of the Emperor Xerxes (who ruled 485–465 B.C.). Once again, the only source for this event is Herodotus. He told how Sataspes was to be executed for a crime when his mother persuaded Xerxes instead to send him on a trip to circumnavigate Africa. Sataspes proceeded in the opposite direction from the one sent by Necho: He sailed west through the Strait of Gibraltar and then down along the northwestern coast of Africa. Herodotus went on:

> After sailing for many months over a vast amount of water and always finding he had to go further, he turned around and made his way back to Egypt. From there he returned to Xerxes and reported that, at the farthest point he reached, he sailed by a dwarf race who wore clothes of palm leaves and fled their villages to the mountains whenever Sataspes and his men went ashore, and that he and his men did them no harm but only went in and took some cattle. But finally, the reason he didn't sail all around Africa was that the ship stopped and just could not go any further.

Upon hearing this excuse for failing to complete his assignment, Xerxes had Sataspes killed after all. Whether true or not, such a tale perhaps says something about the risks assumed by early explorers.

It is noticeable that a number of Greeks have begun to play prominent roles in the history of exploration by this time—Herodotus, Scylax, Alexander the Great. This is no coincidence, as the Persian Empire was about to be challenged by the Greeks, who would bring a whole new dimension to exploration.

4

THE INQUISITIVE GREEKS

The people known to modern English speakers as "Greeks" never called themselves that, and still do not. They call themselves "Hellenes," just as they call their country "Hellas." In ancient times, they occasionally also called themselves "Hellenes," but in general they referred to themselves by the name of the major city-state in which they lived or which dominated their region: Athenians, Corinthians, Spartans, and so on. And in the many centuries before these great city-states arose, if the people identified

Although only one of several Greek city-states, Athens felt it was first among equals and demonstrated it by constructing its great temple, the Parthenon (447–438 B.C.), and other fine buildings. (In the foreground is the Odeon of Herodes Atticus, a theater erected by a wealthy Roman in the late second century A.D. (© Philip Baird www.anthroarcheart.org)

with any large groups, it was with one of the major groups who moved into and throughout the land now known as Greece. What makes their story so amazing, then, is the way these disparate groups managed to shape and share a culture that was so distinctive. In particular, a people and a culture that would show such a modern inquisitiveness about the world at large.

THE EARLY HISTORY OF THE GREEKS

People had been living on the Greek mainland and islands for thousands of years and undoubtedly they would eventually become part of the people and culture to be known as "Greek." But scholars generally agree that the first people who could be called Greeks came from somewhere to the north of Greece about the year 2000 B.C. Little is known of them except that they spoke an Indo-European language that was the ancestor of classical and modern Greek; worshipped a number of gods, among whom a male deity was supreme; and behaved in a relatively aggressive or at least expansive manner. This first wave of Greeks became known as Achaeans, and within a few centuries, they were the dominant people in much of Greece. By about 1650 B.C., Mycenae, their stronghold in the Peloponnesus, the southern portion of Greece, seemed to emerge as the most powerful of the Achaean settlements, and the Achaeans are thus also known as Mycenaeans.

Although not primarily a seagoing people, the Mycenaeans did gradually make their presence felt around the Mediterranean. By about 1500 B.C., they moved over to Crete and took control of the island's centers and economy from the Minoans. They moved on to Cyprus and the southern coast of Turkey and even founded settlements in Syria. Mean-

while, they also ventured westward, trading with the inhabitants of southern Italy, Sicily, Sardinia, and possibly even in Spain. As venturesome as they were, however, the Mycenaeans did not really set forth for new lands; they traveled the well-known routes of the day and they were apparently interested solely in trade. Even the Trojan War—which if it was a historical event was fought principally by the Achaeans—may well have been a war over control of a trade route.

The Trojan War, regarded as the climactic event of this phase of Achaean history, is dated to about 1250 B.C. Within about a century, a new wave of people moved down from the north and began to compete with the Mycenaeans. These people were known as Dorians and, judging from the Greek language they spoke and wrote, they must have been close relatives of the Achaeans. Within a century or two, they had replaced the Mycenaeans as the dominant people in many parts of Greece, and they had also moved onto Crete, Rhodes, southwestern Asia Minor (Turkey), Sicily, and southern Italy. But they were even less of a maritime people than the Mycenaeans, and they do not seem to have sought out any new territories.

It was a third group of people—the Ionians—who seem to have brought the most adventurous and innovative streak to the mix known as "the Greeks." The exact origin of the Ionians remains in dispute, but whoever they were, they appear to have spoken a language close to that of the Achaeans and Dorians. The Ionians may have been resident in the Peloponnesus, and when the Dorians moved in about 1000 B.C., some Ionians apparently fled to Attica, the region where Athens is located, while others fled to the southwestern coast of Turkey. The Ionians who settled on the coast and islands of Turkey would become so prosperous and prominent that they would

The Amber Routes ◠

One of the most prized substances of the ancient world was amber, and in its own way, this "gold of the north" contributed to the ancients' knowledge of new lands. Amber is formed from the resin exuded from certain coniferous trees that grew many millions of years ago; on contact with the air, the resin solidified. When the trees eventually became buried under earth or the sea, the resin changed into the very hard, yellowish-brown, almost translucent lumps known as amber. By far, the largest and finest source of amber in the world is found along the Baltic Sea of northern Europe, from the Jutland peninsula across Poland's coast to Lithuania. Some amber is taken directly from the sea, but most of it is "mined" from a claylike soil known as "blue earth."

Amber has been prized since prehistoric times for its decorative value; some ancients also ascribed symbolic, magical, and curative values to it. It has been found in ancient sites in Mesopotamia and Egypt as well as at the Minoan Palace of Knossos on Crete. But it was the Mycenaean Greeks who really began to import amber into the Mediterranean world in relatively large quantities starting about 1600 B.C. The Greeks who succeeded the Mycenaeans on the mainland and around the Aegean continued to be fascinated by amber. They called it *elektron* and realized that when they rubbed it with a piece of cloth, the amber attracted certain materials. They had in fact discovered what is now called *static electricity,* and the English word *electricity* was deliberately based on the Greek name for amber.

Starting with the Mycenaean Greeks, as the demand for amber grew, several major routes developed for transporting it to the Mediterranean from the Baltic region. Amber from the western end of the Baltic was carried along the coast of northern Europe and over to Britain or Britanny in France; from there it made its way by ship or over land to Spain's Mediterranean coast. Amber from the eastern coast of the Baltic might take an overland route south through Poland, Slovakia, and Slovenia to Aquileia, a port on the head of the Adriatic Sea. From there it would be transported by boat to the Greek mainland and the greater Aegean. Another possibility was to send the amber to the Black Sea, where Greek traders would then transport it to the Aegean. There were two preferred routes to the Black Sea: One followed the Vistula River south through Poland to the Dniester River in Ukraine and down to the Black Sea; another led overland south to the region of modern Vienna, then down the Danube River to the Black Sea.

The reason that amber figures in the history of exploration is that these routes had more than an economic impact. The movements and contacts of the various peoples along these routes led to the spread of knowledge of the geography of Europe—the highest mountains, the best passes, the safest waterways, the best shortcuts, the effect of the seasons, and weather conditions. Various middlemen were involved in the trade of amber between the inhabitants of the Baltic and the Greeks of the Aegean, and this meant that languages and other cultural differences also had to be bridged. Amber thus was one more incentive for the Greeks to explore and discover the world beyond their homeland.

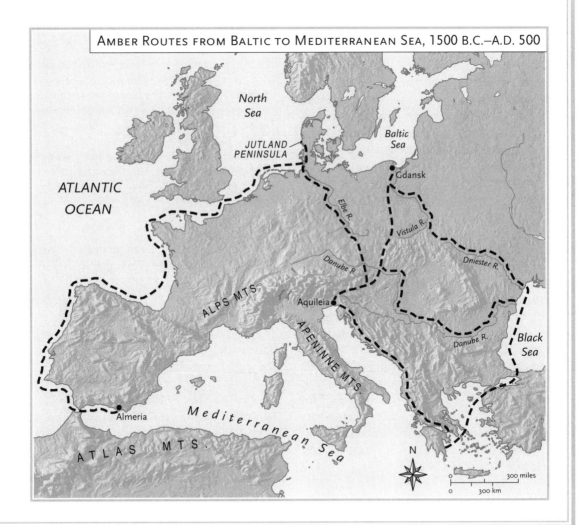

AMBER ROUTES FROM BALTIC TO MEDITERRANEAN SEA, 1500 B.C.–A.D. 500

eventually take the lead over mainland Greeks in various endeavors.

SHARED STORIES

By about 800 B.C., a relatively homogenous culture was emerging on the Greek mainland and on the islands and coastal regions of the Aegean Sea (including the Turkish coast known as Ionia), the culture the people themselves would call "Hellenic." This was based on such elements as the common language, particular techniques and motifs in their arts and crafts, and certain ways of arranging their social, economic, and political systems. Above all, these ancient Greeks shared various myths, legends, and tales that expressed their views of the world and humans' relations with it. Among these were a special variety of stories about heroes who, although descended from gods, performed feats that Greeks recounted as though they were part of their history. Perhaps the best known of these heroes was Herakles (or Hercules, as he was known to the Romans), who performed the 12 labors. Other well-known heroes included Theseus and Perseus.

One of the common themes of the stories of these heroes is that they traveled far and wide around the Mediterranean and even outside its bounds to perform their deeds. Of course, these tales were mythological, but that does not cancel the fact that the ancient Greeks evidently had tremendous curiosity about the world outside their immediate environs. Greek heroic myths, in other words, express the Greeks' willingness both to seek out new lands and to communicate information, however incorrect.

This was especially true with the story of Jason, who was said to have organized an expedition of some 50 men to go in search of the Golden Fleece. Their ship was named the

Rhodes, an island in the southeastern corner of the Mediterranean, was a major participant in the ancient Greek realm. On a rock at the site of Lindos on Rhodes is this carving of the stern of a ship (some 4.6 m long, 5.5 m high), with a lateral rudder and the helmsman's seat visible. It dates from about 180 B.C. and is believed to have been commissioned by sailors to honor both a local official and a local goddess. *(Courtesy of Francesca DiPietro Bowman)*

Argo, so the men were known as the Argonauts. The Golden Fleece had belonged to a ram, or male goat, that had been sacrificed to the god Zeus in a distant land, Colchis, where the fleece was hanging in a grove of trees. Colchis was in the Caucasus region at the far eastern end of the Black Sea, and after sailing there and obtaining the fleece, Jason and the Argonauts made their way back to Greece. Once again, this story, like those of the other heroes, was full of fictional doings, and scholars cannot agree on exactly what real places were being referred to. But it is known that some Greeks had made their way up to the Black Sea by at least 800 B.C., and certainly by 700 B.C. were establishing the first of many colonies they would plant around that sea.

The best known of the shared stories of the ancient Greeks, were the epic poems

The adventures of Odysseus were known wherever Greeks and their culture were present around the Mediterranean. One example is this bronze mirror (about 500 B.C.) from the Etruscan people of Italy, which on its opaque side depicts Odysseus attacking Circe. *(Library of Congress, Prints and Photographs Division [LC-USZ62-110245])*

attributed to Homer, *The Iliad* and *The Odyssey*. Virtually nothing factual is known of Homer as an individual, although it is generally believed that he came from one of the Ionian cities along the coast of present-day Turkey; it is also believed that he wrote down these poems about 750 B.C. Whoever this Homer was, it is quite certain that a large portion of the poems attributed to him had been passed along for several centuries by generations of storytellers.

The Iliad tells the story of the Trojan War and so is largely confined to the locale of Troy. *The Odyssey*, however, recounts the story of the 10-year voyage of Odysseus as he attempts to make his way back to his island home off the northwestern coast of Greece after the Trojan War. Along the way, he has numerous adventures at various exotic locales, and both professional scholars and amateur enthusiasts have never tired of trying to pin these down to specific places. Usually they try to identify Odysseus's locales with sites around the Mediterranean, but some interpret the text as referring to places well outside that sea—as far as Britain—while others place the entire voyage in the Black Sea. Although no one would argue that *The Odyssey* can be treated as a geography text, it is the supreme example of the ancient Greeks' fascination with voyaging into unknown territory. Put another way, it is no wonder that generations of young Greeks raised on *The Odyssey* were inspired to want to set out to see the world.

THE IONIANS

Until about 650 B.C., virtually all peoples on earth chose to explain the world, both known and unknown, by myths, legends, and other imaginative accounts. About then, however, a small number of Greeks began to employ science and mathematics to account for the Earth and its phenomena. These "rationalists" were the Ionian Greeks who lived in cities along the southwestern coast of Turkey, a region that had thus become known as Ionia. As mentioned, there is considerable uncertainty as just who these Ionians were, but there is no question that these people spoke and wrote Greek. One of their major cities was Miletus, and it was one of its citizens, Thales, who lived about 640–546 B.C., used geometry to predict an eclipse of the Sun—a phenomenon that most people attributed to the gods. About 550 B.C., another citizen of Miletus, Anaximander, revolutionized astronomy by claiming that the entire universe was a sphere, with the Earth at the center (although he regarded the Earth as shaped like a cylinder) and the Moon, planets, stars, and Sun encircling it. He used a gnomon, a sundial-like device, to determine the equinoxes, and he was also credited with drawing the first map of the Earth.

That did not survive, but still another Ionian Greek from Miletus, Hecataeus, came along about 500 B.C. and was credited with improving Anaximander's map by providing even more details. Hecataeus is also said to have written two volumes, *Europe* and *Asia*, described as "a journey round the world" and thus gaining for him the epithet "Father of Geography." That should not be taken as proving that he himself traveled widely or meaning that he possessed a solid knowledge of the earth. In fact, as his two books suggest, he believed like most of his Greek contemporaries that there were only the two continents—Africa was regarded as part of Asia. And although Hecataeus thought of the Earth as round, he regarded it is a flat plane, with the two continents surrounded by an ocean.

All these views and versions of the Earth were essentially intellectual—that is, these individuals had apparently arrived at them by collecting information that was brought to them by others and using mathematics and other mental calculations. This approach owed much to the fact that these same Ionian cities were active in sending out mariners, traders, and colonists to distant lands. The port city of Phocaea (near the modern Turkish village of Foca) was among the leaders, and during the 500s B.C., it founded a string of trading stations along the Mediterranean coast, from southern Italy to Spain. Some of the Phocaean settlements grew into prosperous cities; Massalia, the home of Pytheas, the mariner credited with sailing northwestern Europe, was merely the best known of these. The Phocaean also founded settlements up along both shores of the Adriatic Sea, between eastern Italy and Yugoslavia.

The Phocaean also had a settlement on the Black Sea, but the Ionians of Miletus were far more active in exploring and settling the Black Sea. The Roman historian, Pliny, told a story of Midacritus, an Ionian Greek most likely from Phocaea, "who was the first to import 'white lead' [that is, tin] from the Tin Island." It is not clear what this refers to, but it would seem that Pliny was claiming that this Midacritus sailed all the way to Cornwall, in Britain, the same destination of Pytheas. The Greeks who went off to establish these settlements may not have been heroes like the Argonauts, and they were probably motivated primarily by the desire to improve their own lot in life.

OTHER GREEKS, OTHER JOURNEYS

Ionians were not the only Greeks active in exploring distant lands between 650 and 400 B.C. Scylax has already been mentioned: He was the mariner commissioned by the Persian King Darius to lead an expedition to India and the Persian Gulf. Scylax was from Caria, a region just south of the Ionian Greek region,

and if not a Greek himself, was probably influenced by the expansive Ionian Greeks. There was even the story—although told only by the later Greek historian Pausanias—that another citizen of Caria, Euphemus, was blown by the winds through the Strait of Gibraltar and all across the great ocean to an island inhabited by red-skinned men with horses' tails; some people have tried to claim that this indicates that some ancient got all the way to the Antilles (in the Caribbean!), but no scholars accept this.

Herodotus, the Greek historian, told of a mariner named Colaeus, who about 640 B.C. was trying to sail from the coast of North Africa back to his island home of Samos, off the coast of Turkey. Heavy winds instead blew him west all the way across the Mediterranean and outside the Strait of Gibraltar to the land of Tartessus, located on the southwestern coast of Spain. There Colaeus is said to have picked up such a large load of silver that, when he got back to Samos, he was able to retire.

Then there was a tale about a certain sea captain from Massalia, the same Greek colony that was home port to Pytheas, who was said by a later Roman author, Festus Rufus Avienus, to have written a periplus (literally, "sailing-round," basically a guide to coastal settlements) about 525 B.C. In this periplus, the Massalian mariner shows a good knowledge of the coast of Spain and also refers to the British Isles and even to Ireland, but since the Roman Avienus is the only one ever to refer to this periplus, it is not clear just how much credence should be given it. And there was still another Massalian, Euthymenes, who about 530 B.C. was said to have sailed out through the Strait of Gibraltar and down along the west coast of Africa. There he came to a large river in which he saw crocodiles—which Euthymenes believed indicated he had seen

Lost Atlantis

One of the most enduring yet astounding contributions of the ancient Greeks to the discovery of new lands is in fact a complete fiction: the tale of Lost Atlantis. The story began with the famous Greek philosopher Plato (429–347 B.C.), who in two of his works, the *Timaeus* and the *Critias,* told of a story allegedly passed on to Greeks by an Egyptian priest. The priest said Atlantis had existed 9,000 years before ancient Athens and that the island was located in the great ocean outside the Pillars of Hercules—that is, the Strait of Gibraltar.

This Atlantis was a highly advanced and prosperous land. Among its more remarkable features were quantities of gold, ambitious canals, plentiful fruits and flowers, great palaces, a horse-racing track, and wild bulls that were hunted down. Atlantis was purportedly the center of an empire that dominated much of the Mediterranean world until Athens rose up and defeated it. After that, violent earthquakes and floods overwhelmed Atlantis, and in one day the whole island sank to the depths of the ocean.

Most of the ancients who commented on Plato's story of Atlantis recognized it as a fiction intended to convey a moral: The pursuit of excessive material possessions and power would only lead to the destruction of a society. Some ancients, however, did seem to take it literally. They might be excused for not knowing that, in 9000 B.C., human beings were barely emerging from the Stone Age. But they should have been suspicious that such a large landmass could have sunk in one day; according to the tale, the capital city of Atlantis alone had an area greater than all of Greece!

For many centuries, Atlantis was simply a name occasionally discussed by scholarly writers. With the Europeans' discovery of the Americas, however, Atlantis suddenly emerged as though it were a real place. One or another of the newly found American islands or the complete American continent was nominated as Atlantis—somehow the fact that Atlantis was to have sunk beneath the waves was overlooked. And in the five centuries since 1492, various writers have continued to nominate locales all over the earth as the site of Atlantis. The list of books dealing with Atlantis since 1492 fills many pages; many of these books are serious discussions of geology, geography, and other scientific disciplines.

the Upper Nile. (Modern scholars believe it is the Senegal River that was being described.)

Nothing about these tales can be verified, but as with all such stories that the ancient Greeks recounted, what matters is the message between the lines: The Greeks knew the risks of setting out to sea but were intrigued by the prospects of traveling far afield.

TWO ADVENTUROUS GREEKS

Perhaps no one epitomized this spirit of the ancient Greeks more than Herodotus, a Greek from another city of Caria, Hallicarnassus. Born about 484 B.C., he traveled widely in his youth, not only in Greece, but also in Meso-

Then in the 20th century, a new twist was added to this story: actual expeditions—some costing large sums of money and involving professional scientists—set forth to points all over the world to search for Atlantis. To this day, every few years another "explorer" claims to have found the actual remains of Atlantis. So it is that this ancient Greek tale has stimulated centuries of discussions that have contributed in some degree to exploring and revealing disputed parts of the world.

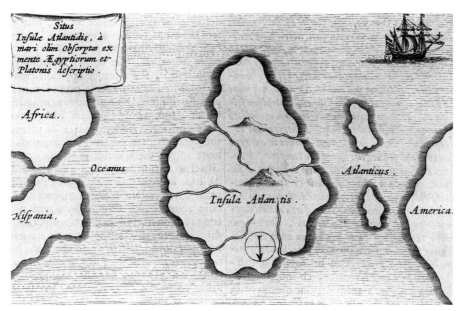

Atlantis was the creation of the Greek philosopher Plato, but people across the centuries have chosen to treat it as a real place. In this map from a book of 1665, Atlantis is shown as a large island between Europe and North America. *(Library of Congress, Prints and Photographs Division [LC-USZ62-76292])*

potamia, the Phoenician coast, Egypt, the eastern coast of North Africa, and all the way to southwest Russia. He visited Athens in 447 B.C., and by 443 B.C. he had moved to a new Greek colony in southern Italy. By then he was writing a history of the world up to his time, with emphasis on the wars between the Persians and the Greeks (499–479 B.C.). But Herodotus's history was much more than what is understood by that word today. In addition to the historical narrative, it is a vast encyclopedia of geographical facts gained firsthand or from his research, observations on human beings encountered or described, quotations from major writers and obscure sources, tales of the most commonplace and the most fantastic.

Herodotus was called "the Father of History" by the great Greek philosopher Aristotle, but he might also be called the first true explorer. Almost no individual earlier than Herodotus comes into focus with such an insatiable curiosity about the world at large.

Herodotus, a Greek from Hallicarnassus in what is today southwestern Turkey, traveled widely before arriving in Athens in 447 B.C.—the very year construction of the Parthenon, shown here, began. He would not stay to see it completed, but he would have been inspired by the Athenians to continue writing about the accomplishments of his fellow Greeks. *(Library of Congress, Prints and Photographs Division [LC-USZ62-94169])*

He not only traveled widely, he collected every bit of information he could about the places he visited and those he was only told about.

Many of the stories about the early explorers are known only because Herodotus collected them. Many places in distant parts—southwest Russia, for example, or lower Egypt—were barely known about until Herodotus reported on them. And he did so in an engaging, flexible style that made his information accessible to any literate person. True, Herodotus repeated all kinds of fabulous tales, but there are also elements in his work that sound like thoroughly modern scholarship. Below Herodotus tells of how he learned much about Egypt from the priests he met at Egyptian temples:

> Those of their narrations that I heard with regard to the gods, I am not anxious to relate in full, but I shall mention them only because I consider that all men are equally ignorant of these matters: and whatever things of them I may record I shall record only because I am compelled by the course of the story. [The priests] said also that the first man who became king of Egypt was Min; and that in his time all Egypt except the district of Thebes was a swamp, and none of the regions were then above water which now lie below the lake of Moiris, to which lake it is a voyage of seven days up the river from the sea. I thought that they said well about the land, for it is manifestly true even to a person who has not heard it beforehand but has only seen, at least if he have understanding, that the Egypt to which the Hellenes come in ships is a land that has been won by the Egyptians as an addition, and that it is a gift of the river.

Egypt—"the gift of the [Nile] river": No one has ever said it better in all the centuries since Herodotus. After talking with the priests, like a true explorer he set out to learn about the source of the Nile and its annual flooding, but

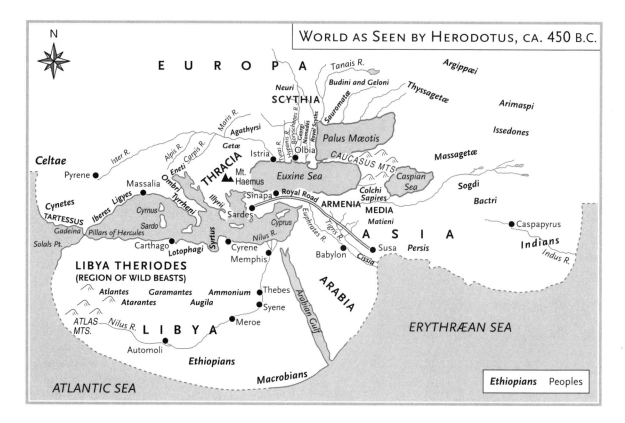

WORLD AS SEEN BY HERODOTUS, CA. 450 B.C.

N

EUROPA

Tanais R.

Argippœi

Neuri

Budini and Geloni

Thyssagetæ

Arimaspi

SCYTHIA

Sauromatæ

Borysthenes R.

Georgi
Nomades
Royal Scyths

Hypanis R.

Issedones

Maris R.

Agathyrsi

Palus Mæotis

Massagetæ

Celtae

Ister R.

Alpis R.

Carpis R.

Getæ

Istria

Olbia

CAUCASUS MTS.

Caspian
Sea

Sogdi

Pyrene

Eneti

THRACIA

Mt.
Haemus

Euxine Sea

Massalia

Ombri

Illyrii

Sinapa

Royal Road

Colchi
Sapires

Bactri

Cynetes

Iberes

Ligyes

Tyrrheni

Cyrnus

Sardes

Cyprus

ARMENIA

MEDIA

Matieni

TARTESSUS

Sardo

Euphrates R.

Tigris R.

ASIA

Caspapyrus

Gadeina

Pillars of Hercules

Syrtis

Nilus R.

Persis

Indians

Solals Pt.

Carthago

Lotophagi

Cyrene

Cyrene

Babylon

Cissia

Susa

Indus R.

Memphis

LIBYA THERIODES
(REGION OF WILD BEASTS)

ARABIA

Atlantes

Garamantes

Ammonium

Thebes

ERYTHRÆAN SEA

Atarantes

Augila

Syene

ATLAS
MTS.

Nilus R.

LIBYA

Meroe

Arabian Gulf

Automoli

Ethiopians

ATLANTIC SEA

Macrobians

| *Ethiopians* | Peoples |

he eventually concluded: "[A]bout the sources of the Nile, no one, whether Egyptian or Libyan or Greek, who has talked with me, has admitted that he knew anything, except the clerk of the holy utensil at the shrine of Athene in Sais in Egypt; but I think he was joking when he said he knew accurately."

Herodotus is believed to have died about 424 B.C., and just a few years before this, about 430 B.C., another remarkable Greek was born. Xenophon was an Athenian aristocrat and military man, and in 401 B.C. he accepted an invitation from the Persian Cyrus the Younger to join a military campaign that turned out to be an attempt to overthrow Cyrus's older brother, Artaxerxes, king of Persia. Some 10,000 Greek mercenaries eventually joined this expedition, and when Cyrus was killed in

the battle of Cunaxa in Mesopotamia, Xenophon eventually assumed command of this Greek army and led them on their retreat from the Persians. Their six-month journey took them some 800 miles from near Baghdad all the way to the Black Sea, and often they had to fight off hostile forces. It was an epic feat but might have gone unnoticed had not Xenophon eventually written a stirring account of it, the *Anabasis*—the Greek meaning "a military movement" but usually translated as "The Retreat of the 10,000."

After they made their way north and out of Mesopotamia, these Greeks moved across the regions known today as Kurdistan and Turkish Armenia. It appears that they reached the source of the Tigris River and passed near the source of the Euphrates; they were close to

Lake Van. During the winter weeks, they found themselves in the rugged mountains, and many died from the cold and exhaustion. Finally they arrived at a mountain peak, and Xenophon described this event in one of the best known passages in Greek history:

> No sooner had the men in the lead ascended it and caught sight of the sea than a great cry arose. Xenophon, in the rear, catching the sound of it, assumed that another group of enemies must be attacking. . . . But as the shout became louder and nearer, and those who from time to time came up from the rear began racing at full speed toward the shouting, and the shout-

ing continued at still greater volume as the numbers increased, Xenophon realized that something extraordinary must have occurred, so he mounted his horse and taking his cavalry with him, galloped to the rescue. Presently they could hear the soldiers shouting and passing on the joyful word, "The sea! The sea!"

Xenophon never saw himself as an explorer, not even a geographer; he wrote his account as an historian; but he was so observant and so graphic that his *Anabasis* served to introduce a whole new region to his fellow Greeks. That is not to say that they knew nothing about parts of the region. Nor does it mean that it is absolutely clear just where Xenophon and his army traveled, although modern scholars have pretty much agreed on the route. The point, though, is that this very sophisticated man wrote an account that demonstrated both honesty about a near disastrous expedition and objective descriptions of a little-known region.

Consider a typical passage from the *Anabasis.* where the Greeks have captured a group of men in northern Mesopotamia and are wondering what lies ahead:

There are no contemporary portraits of Xenophon, any more than of the other ancient Greeks still so admired. This portrait from 1810 is really an idealized tribute to this general/adventurer/author whose account of his epic trek across the Middle East helped to introduce that region to the ancient Europeans. *(Library of Congress, Prints and Photographs Division [LC-USZ61-1366])*

> After hearing the statements of the prisoners, the Greek officers seated apart those who claimed to have any special knowledge of the country in any direction. They sat them apart without making it clear which particular route they intended to take. Finally they decided that they must force a passage through the hills into the territory of the Kurds; according to what their informants told them, when they had once passed these, they would find themselves in Armenia—the rich and large territory governed by Orontas—and from Armenia it would be easy to proceed in any direction.

Thereupon they offered sacrifice so as to be ready to start on the march as soon as the right moment arrived. Their chief fear was that the high pass over the mountains might be occupied in advance.

This is a far cry from the mythological versions of adventures and exotic lands that most ancient peoples were accustomed to.

THE GREEKS' LIMITED KNOWLEDGE

As it happened, at the same time that Xenophon was fighting alongside Cyrus at the Battle of Cunaxa, another Greek was aiding Cyrus's brother, King Artaxerxes. This was Ctesias, a physician from Cnidos, yet another Greek colony on the southwest coast of Turkey. The Persians had controlled this part of southwest Asia since 546 B.C., and it was quite common for Greeks to cooperate with the Persians. Little is known about Ctesias, and none of his writings have survived in their original texts, but it is clear from other ancient authors that he was famed for a history of India that he had written. Ctesias's so-called history was hardly what would qualify as history today; it was clearly little more than a collection of tales that he heard while at the Persian court, for the Persians did have dealings with India. Another ancient writer, Dionysus of Halicarnassus, characterized Ctesis's work as "entertaining but badly composed." Ctesias did not even claim to have visited India, and the land he describes is full of the exotic and fabulous, although it is possible that some of what he claims is based on misunderstandings. For instance, Ctesias says that, in India, there dwell some people who have only one very large foot—so big they can use it as a sunshade. Some scholars suggest that Ctesias simply misunderstood reports of the practice of certain Indian holy men who stood in unusual poses for a long time, usually on one foot.

Ctesias may be an extreme example of the Greeks' misconceptions of the world during the classic age, but there is no denying that most ancient Greeks' descriptions of the world were rife with errors. For all their travels, for all their research, for all their attempts at objective description, they simply did not know enough about the world beyond their own immediate environs—primarily, the lands surrounding the Mediterranean Sea. This would change with the contributions of the man who came to be known as Alexander the Great.

5

ALEXANDER THE GREAT AND THE HELLENISTIC WORLD

The ancient Greeks, for all their accomplishments, were in fact limited in their knowledge of the world at large. Partly this was because it was simply not that easy to obtain and communicate facts about the world beyond one's immediate region: A ship captain might return from some distant land and describe unusual sights, but such tales would not have carried far. Partly, too, it was because the ancient Greeks had a certain smugness, a sense of superiority: They felt they had the most civilized, the most sophisticated society, so there was no great need to rush off to seek out new places. This is reflected in their word for non-Greek speakers—*barbaros:* Believed to be derived from the sound of the languages spoken by non-Greeks, it came to mean foreign, crude, ignorant. Since the non-Greek world was inhabited by "barbarians," the Greeks believed that there was not much to be gained from them.

North of the main Greek city-states, for example, was a vast territory known as Macedon—a region now divided up among modern Greece, the Former Yugoslavian Republic of Macedonia, and Bulgaria. A raw, mountainous land, most of it was as shadowy as its inhabitants. Even today, scholars are not absolutely clear about just who the ancient Macedonians were—that is, their ethnic origins and relationships—and the ancient Greeks of the centuries just tended to regard them as at least semi-barbarians.

In fact, although Macedon long remained a rather primitive society compared to the great city-states of Greece, many Macedonians spoke a form of Greek and their leaders claimed to share Greek culture. When Philip II took over the throne of Macedon in 359 B.C., he asserted his "Greekness" by setting about to conquer the Greek city-states. By 336 he had accomplished this and was preparing to lead a combined Macedonian-Greek invasion

These gold coins portray Philip II, king of Macedonia from 382–336 B.C. and father of Alexander the Great. It was Philip who succeeded in conquering the city-states of Greece. He died before he could undertake his plan to invade the Persian Empire, a goal his son attained. *(Library of Congress, Prints and Photographs Division [LC-USZ62-107427])*

of Persia when he was assassinated. His 20-year-old son, Alexander, immediately assumed the throne. In the short life left to him, Alexander accomplished so much that he would go down in history as one of the few individuals always identified as "the great." Although this usually is taken to refer to his military feats, the case can be made that the same word characterizes his role in the history of exploration.

ALEXANDER THE WARRIOR

There are several authentic texts about Alexander by his contemporaries, but they are known only from later works that quote them. Probably many of the tales told of Alexander were of the legendary kind attributed to such celebrated heroes, but there was probably at least a grain of truth behind them. For instance, it was claimed that when he heard about his father's conquests of the Greek city-states, he cried, saying, "My father will leave nothing great for me to do." He was said to have carried a copy of Homer's *Iliad* with him at all times because he so admired the warrior-hero Achilles. It was also said that his favorite horse, Bucephalus, was one that no one else had dared to try to tame.

Whether Alexander was such a superhuman person or not, he was an extraordinarily gifted individual. When he was 13 years old, his parents engaged the Greek philosopher Aristotle to come to Macedonia to tutor him. Aristotle was an equally extraordinary person, in command of the entire range of human knowledge at that time. He taught Alexander the great classics and ideals of Greek culture and also about the countries and peoples elsewhere in the known world as well as the natural history of the plants and animals around them. By the time he became king, then, Alexander was not only a brave and vigorous young man, he was an intelligent and inquisitive one.

His first acts as king were to extend his rule over some of the tribes north of Macedonia and to put down a revolt in the Greek city-state of Thebes—and then sell most of its 30,000 citizens into slavery. After this, the rest of the Greek city-states, including Athens, acknowledged Alexander's leadership, and by the spring of 334 B.C. he was ready to pursue the goal his father had in mind before he was killed—to conquer the Persian Empire. With an army of some 35,000 Macedonians, Greeks, and foreign mercenaries, he crossed the Hellespont, the ancient Greeks' name for the Strait of Dardanelles that separated Europe from Asia in what is modern Turkey.

In the next four years, Alexander led his often-outnumbered troops in a series of battles and sieges that routed the Persian armies and conquered all the major cities of the Persian Empire. These included the Phoenician port city of Tyre (in modern Lebanon), the Egyptian city of Memphis, the Mesopotamian city of Babylon (in modern Iraq), and the Persian capital city of Persepolis (in modern Iran). While in Egypt, he founded the

An early 19th-century print of the remains of ancient Tyre, the prosperous Phoenician port-city on the Mediterranean coast of what is now southern Lebanon. Alexander began a siege of Tyre in early 322 B.C., but it took some seven months and tremendous efforts before he conquered it. *(Library of Congress, Prints and Photographs Division [LC-USZC4-3489])*

first of many cities he would establish, Alexandria, along the Mediterranean coast, destined to become one of the great cities of the ancient world.

ALEXANDER THE EXPLORER

After he conquered Persepolis—and burnt it, according to legend, to pay back the Persians for having burnt Athens in 480 B.C.—Alexander released the many Greeks who wanted to go home. Which again says something about the Greeks' attitude toward the world at large. They had now traversed the world that they knew about; beyond lay the unknown—and these Greeks were not interested in exploring this "barbarian" world.

But Alexander was, and during the next five years he led a mixed army of Macedonians and mercenaries from several lands in one of the most amazing expeditions of all time.

True, Alexander's immediate goal was to pursue rival rulers and to conquer more lands. But to accomplish what he did, he had to be motivated by something beyond the mere desire to win battles and acquire land. In any case, the expedition earns its place in the history of exploration because Alexander—faithful to his tutor, Aristotle—took along a number of scientists to observe and record all that was new. And although much of the land traversed was inhabited, it rates as an expedition of discovery because it was the reports of several of Alexander's staff that brought this

The Khyber Pass on the border of Afghanistan and Pakistan, some 30 miles long, provides a relatively easy route through the Safed Koh Mountains. It has been the main land approach to India from Central Asia and the west since ancient times, and it was chosen by Alexander the Great for his entry into northern India. (© Philip Baird www.anthroarcheart.org)

vast region of Asia into the consciousness of the Western world.

This was not just some vague notion of an exotic region. The famous historian-geographer Herodotus, for instance, writing some 100 years before Alexander's expedition, had described some of the geographical features and peoples of this part of the world, but he based everything on secondhand reports and was usually way off the mark. Alexander took with him some *bematists* (Greek for "pacers"), meaning surveyors, who not only measured the distances of the routes but also recorded the peoples and products along the way.

Alexander set out from Persepolis in the spring of 330 B.C. and led his army north through the Zagros Mountains into the region known as Media. He then proceeded along the southern shore of the Caspian Sea—which he mistakenly came to believe was an ocean gulf—eastward through the region known as Parthia. After turning down into southeastern Persia, he headed north into Afghanistan; at one point he crossed a mountain pass at some 8,700 feet, where his troops suffered greatly from the cold and snow.

After spending the winter in northern Afghanistan (near the location of modern Kabul), he set out in the spring of 329 B.C. and crossed the mountain range known as the Hindu Kush into regions known as Bactria and Sogdiana. There he crossed the great Oxus River (now the Amu Darya) and went on to another great river, the Jaxartes (now the Syr Darya), where he founded a city to mark the farthest point he would reach in Central Asia.

Alexander was now determined to invade and conquer India, and in the spring of 327 B.C. he set out southward. One part of his army entered India through what is now the famous Khyber Pass, but Alexander led another force through mountains so remote and wild that it would be another 2,220 years before there was

This 19th-century painting is an artist's version of Alexander's forces attacking the fortress of Aornus near the upper Indus River. Situated on an almost inaccessible rocky prominence, the fort was taken by Alexander in the spring of 326 B.C. *(Library of Congress, Prints and Photographs Division [LC-USZ62-93890])*

any record of an explorer visiting them. He joined up with his other troops on the banks of the Indus River (in what is now Pakistan), where he rested over the winter before crossing over into the region known as the Punjab. There, in spring 326 B.C., Alexander led his troops against the Fortress of Aornus, high on a rock, and in a seemingly impossible feat, defeated the Indian tribesmen who had taken refuge there. He then proceeded to defeat the most powerful prince in northwestern India at a battle near the Hydaspes River. (His beloved horse, Bucephalus, died after this battle, so Alexander founded the city of Bucephala on the site.)

Alexander intended to march still further south and conquer more of India, but his troops refused to go any farther. So Alexander had his men build a small fleet of ships and then, with about half his troops marching along both sides of the Indus River and the rest in the ships, he led his army down to the Indus Delta on the Arabian Sea. Along the way they were amazed by some of the exotic vegetation they saw, such as the great banyan trees, which one of his companions, Onesicritus, described in his account of the trip:

> The branches. . . . grow downwards until they touch the earth; after which they spread underground and take root like layers and then spring up and grow into a stem; after that again. . . . they are bent down and form first one and then another layer, and so on continuously so that from one tree proceeds a long sunshade, resembling a tent supported by many poles, . . . the trees are of such a size that five men can with difficulty clasp their trunks.

Alexander now faced the challenge of getting his men back to Babylon, the city that he had chosen to be the capital of his new empire in Asia. Well before reaching the sea, he had already sent one section of his army—led by Craterus—across western India and southern Persia (Iran). He now divided his remaining forces into two groups. He would lead one group westward overland, but the other stayed with the ships they had built to sail down the Indus. This fleet, commanded by a Cretan-Greek admiral, Nearchus, sailed all the way along the coasts of the Arabian Sea and the Persian Gulf until reaching its head and the mouth of the Euphrates River. This voyage itself ranks as one of the great maritime voyages of the ancient world—some 1,400 miles through largely unknown waters and along an unknown coast. Nearchus himself wrote a thorough account, and although it was lost, a quite complete summary survived in the work of Arrian, a Roman of the second century A.D. who also wrote the best account of the life of Alexander.

Many of Nearchus's detailed descriptions can be easily assigned to known places today—Karachi in Pakistan, Ormuz in Iran. He also described the many unusual encounters during the five months they were either sailing or seeking food and water on shore. At one point, they had to fight off some 600 "savages," and Nearchus described those they took captive:

> They were hairy over their heads as well as the rest of their persons and had fingernails like wild beasts; at least they were said to use their nails like iron tools and to kill fish by tearing with them and to cut up woods of the softer sorts. . . . For clothing they wore the skins of wild beats, some indeed wearing the thick skins of the bigger fish.

On another occasion, according to Arrian's account:

> Nearchus says they saw in the east water blown up from the sea, as though it were carried along by the blast of a whirlwind, and the men, being terrified, enquired of their guides what this was . . . They replied that these were whales. . . . whereupon the sailors were seized with panic and dropped the oars from their hands. Nearchus went up to his men and cheered and inspired

them and as he passed them in his own vessel he bade them draw up their ships in line as if for a naval engagement and row forward in close array and with much noise, accompanying with loud shouts the plashing of their oars. At this they took heart and advanced all together at a signal and when they came near the monsters of the deep they shouted with all their might and blew their trumpets and made all possible noise with their oars . . . on hearing which the whales . . . took fright and plunged into the depths, but not long after came to the sur-

face again close to the sterns of the vessels and once more spouted great jets of sea water.

Nearchus and his ships and crews eventually sailed up to the heads of the Persian Gulf and made their way up the Tigris River and soon rejoined Alexander, who had made his way across southern Persia and then into Mesopotamia. His trip, which had taken about the same five months, had its own challenges, for it led through uncharted and rugged territory, aggravated by the extreme heat and con-

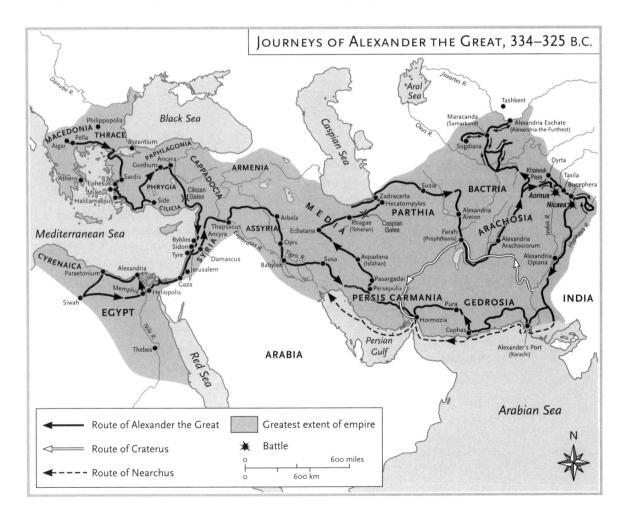

JOURNEYS OF ALEXANDER THE GREAT, 334–325 B.C.

stant shortages of food and water. With those men still with him—he had lost thousands of men along the way and thousands of others had chosen to stay behind—Alexander made his way to Babylon, arriving there in early 324 B.C.

ALEXANDER'S LEGACY:
The Hellenistic World

It had been a truly fabulous six years since Alexander had set out from Persepolis, years in which he not only fought a number of major battles, killed or displaced a number of Persian and other leaders, founded some 70 outposts and cities, and overcame the most difficult physical obstacles imaginable. Through the writings of several of his companions, he would throw light on a vast part of the earth that had been consigned to darkness. And once established at Babylon, Alexander set about introducing some order into his far-flung empire. He also was said to have planned to lead a sailing expedition around Arabia and Africa, but before he could do this, he died of malaria in June 323 B.C. Alexander left behind one son, but he was only an infant, so Alexander's generals began to share in governing the empire. By 311 B.C., however, they had taken to quarreling so much that they split up the empire into three kingdoms.

The Lighthouse and Library of Alexandria

Under Ptolemy I and his successors in the Ptolemaic Dynasty, the Egyptian port city of Alexandria soon developed into one of the major cities of the ancient world, a center of both international trade and cosmopolitan culture. Prominence in these two areas was embodied in Alexandria's two great structures—the lighthouse (one of the Seven Wonders of the Ancient World) and the library. The lighthouse, designed by a Greek, Sostratos, was some 440 feet high and stood on an islet in the harbor. A continually burning fire provided the light that could be seen far at sea by the many ships approaching the city with their goods—and tales—from all over the world. Erected about 270 B.C., it collapsed during an earthquake about A.D. 730. The library, established by Ptolemy I but greatly expanded by his son, provided another window on the world: It gradually collected copies of virtually every existing written work known. These were in the form of scrolls, most of them made of papyrus, the early form of paper, and also some of parchment, made of animal skin. But the great library of Alexandria was more than a depository of written works; it was also a center of scholarly and scientific studies. Its succession of distinguished chief librarians, its staff, the permanent and transient scholars who used its resources—eventually estimated to have reached 700,000 scrolls—made this the premier center of knowledge about the world for several centuries. Some ancients blamed Julius Caesar for destroying a large part of it when he besieged the city in 47 B.C., but most scholars now agree that it was destroyed over a long period of time and during several attacks on the city.

Alexander's accomplishments and legacy did not vanish. Not only had he established those many outposts and cities, he had imposed Greek and Macedonian rulers over much of the territory that he had conquered. Many of his Greek and Macedonian soldiers had simply stayed behind to make new lives in these distant lands. The Greek language, Greek ideas of society, Greek culture, Greek commerce—they were now pervasive from the old Greek colonies at the far western Mediterranean such as Massalia to the new outposts in Central Asia and northern India. This phase of history is known as the Hellenistic Age—for the Greeks called themselves "Hellenes"—and is regarded as lasting from the time of Alexander until the Romans took over most of this realm about 200 years later.

The Hellenistic Age was characterized not just by the prominence of Greek ideas and culture. There was a more cosmopolitan spirit to this period, brought about by the diversity of peoples and activities now moving about this vast area. There was an openness to new ideas, new places, new ways of doing things. Pytheas, the Greek from Massalia who sailed into the north Atlantic, was one example of this new spirit. Perhaps the most outstanding symbol of the Hellenistic Age was, fittingly, a city founded by Alexander himself—Alexandria, on the Mediterranean Sea at the western edge of the Nile Delta. With the breakup of Alexander's empire, one of his Macedonian generals, Ptolemy, made this port city the capital of his new kingdom based in Egypt.

THE PTOLEMIES SUPPORT EXPLORATION

Ptolemy, who had accompanied Alexander all the way to the Indus River and back, took up Alexander's idea of an expedition to Arabia. During his reign (323–285 B.C.), he sponsored an expedition under an admiral Philo, who sailed down along the Africa side of the Arabian Sea. Philo did not discover any new lands, but following his return the Egyptians under Ptolemy began to import elephants and ivory from Africa south of Egypt. Ptolemy I's son and successor, Ptolemy II Philadelphus, established trading ports along the Red Sea, opened up trade with Yemen and Somalia, and sent expeditions that explored the coast of the Horn of Africa. Subsequent members of the Ptolemaic Dynasty, as these rulers of Egypt are known, sent still more expeditions to this region.

Admittedly, these expeditions were more concerned with trade, but each contact increased the store of knowledge of these little-known locales. One of the most ambitious explorers of this era was a man who seemed to have combined commercial goals with sheer curiosity, Eudoxus of Cyszicus, a city in northwest Turkey. The adventures of Eudoxus are known only through the account in Strabo, the Greek geographer and historian (ca. 63 B.C.–ca. A.D. 24), who in turn was simply repeating the account of Posidonius (ca. 135–50 B.C.), another Greek-Roman historian. Eudoxus's first expedition took place under Ptolemy VIII Euergetes II, who ruled the kingdom from 146 to 111 B.C. As the story went, "an Indian happened to be brought to the king by the guards of the Arabian [Gulf], who said they found him cast ashore alone and half dead, but who he was and whence he came they did not know because they could not understand his language." After the Indian was taught Greek, "he promised to be a guide on a voyage to India for men chosen by the king." Eudoxus is among those who went but when he returned loaded with precious stones and other valuable objects, Euergetes took all (or most of) his cargo. When Euergetes died, his widow sponsored another expedition to India; again, Eudoxus returned with valuable goods, again, the new king, seized all (or most all) of his cargo.

One would think that Eudoxus would quit at that, but while returning on that second voyage, he had been blown ashore on the east coast of Africa. Not having any notion of how large Africa was, he decided to sail around it and head straight for India, thus avoiding the Ptolemies—by heading first for its west (Atlantic) coast. He fitted out a ship and sailed across the Mediterranean, along the way taking on all kinds of cargo expected to trade in Africa and India, "and also physicians. . . . and carpenters besides." Sailing through the Pillars of Hercules, he rounded the northwest shoulder of Africa, but before long his ship ran aground and was wrecked. He built a new ship and sailed a bit farther, but then turned back, intending to make a new voyage in a larger ship. In fact, Eudoxus probably had gone only slightly south of Morocco.

On his way back "he saw and noted down a well-watered and well-wooded but unpeopled island"—possibly one of the Canaries, possibly one of the Madeiras. After several adventures in northwest Africa, he made his way back to Spain, built two more ships, and organized yet another expedition with the goal of reaching India. Even Strabo remarks: "How was it that [Eudoxus] did not fear. . . . to sail again." In any case, he sailed off once more into the Atlantic and down the west coast of Africa—and was never heard of again. Although some scholars question just how much of Eudoxus's story is true, others accept it and regard Eudoxus as having earned a place in the history of exploration.

THE LEGACY OF OTHER GREEKS

The Ptolemaic dynasty ruled Egypt, but the rest of Alexander's vast empire was divided up among several of his former generals and their heirs. One of these was Seleucus I Nicator, who by 312 B.C. assumed control of the territory that included Mesopotamia and Persia. He extended his rule west to the Mediterranean and east all the way to the upper Indus Valley of India, where Alexander had left behind a relatively weak Macedonian-Greek colonial administration. Seleucus, of Greek-Macedonian descent, although a tough military man, was also interested in knowing more about the world he lived in—to exploit it, of course. About 285 B.C., he sent a man named Patrocles on an expedition to the Caspian Sea. Patrocles sailed along the southern edge of the sea, noting the various rivers that entered there, and then sailed eastward out of the sea on a since dried-up gulf. He returned with claims that the Caspian Sea opened into a northern ocean and that it also was connected by a water route to India, misunderstandings that would mislead the Greeks for some time to come.

Meanwhile, an Indian by the name of Chandragupta Maurya had seized power in northeastern India, and by about 305 B.C. he had forced Seleucus to cede him control over the region once occupied by Alexander's forces. Chandragupta established a new capital at Pataliputra on the Ganges River, and Seleucus, wanting to maintain good relations with his neighbor, in 302 B.C. sent an ambassador there. He chose Megasthenes, a Greek of considerable learning, who ended up writing the *Indica*, a complete account of India—its geography, climate, government, people, customs, and religion.

Once again, the original text has not survived, but large parts of it were preserved in the texts of other ancient authors, including Strabo and Arrian, who have previously been cited as preserving so much about Alexander. The *Indica* was for many centuries the most

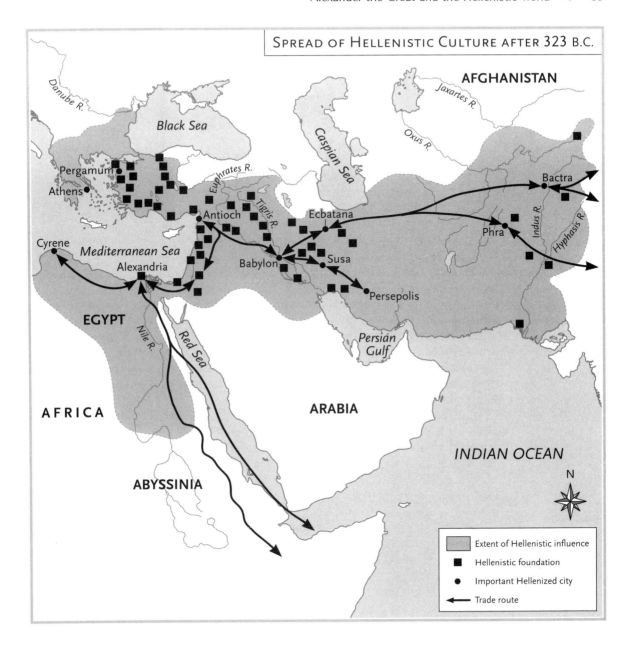

SPREAD OF HELLENISTIC CULTURE AFTER 323 B.C.

AFGHANISTAN

Jaxartes R.

Oxus R.

Black Sea

Danube R.

Pergamum
Athens

Bactra

Euphrates R.

Antioch

Tigris R.

Ecbatana

Caspian Sea

Phra

Indus R.

Hyphasis R.

Cyrene

Mediterranean Sea

Alexandria

Babylon

Susa

Persepolis

EGYPT

Nile R.

Red Sea

Persian Gulf

AFRICA

ARABIA

INDIAN OCEAN

ABYSSINIA

N

Extent of Hellenistic influence
Hellenistic foundation
Important Hellenized city
Trade route

respected work on India in the West, and modern scholars, by comparing his statements with those of Indian accounts of that time, have confirmed that Megasthenes was far more accurate than most of his contemporaries. He knew, for instance, that the Indus River flowed from northeast to southwest; that the Ganges also started in that direction but then turned eastward; that the Himalaya range ran across the northern boundary of

The Greek Geographers

Beyond their role in leading expeditions to distant lands, the ancient Greeks had a strong tradition of what might be called "intellectual journeying." That is, they were among the first to speculate about, calculate, and describe the true nature of the earth. The first to claim that the earth was a complete sphere seem to have been followers of the Greek philosopher and mathematician Pythagoras. A rather mysterious figure, he was born about 580 B.C. and eventually settled in southern Italy, where he evidently taught that the Earth was spherical. (None of his writings have survived.) Another Greek, Heraclides Ponticus, born about 388 B.C. at one of the Greek colonies on the Black Sea, seems to have been the first to claim that the earth revolved around its axis, not that the stars were moving around the Earth. Still another Greek, Aristarchus from the island of Samos, actually suggested that the earth revolved around the Sun.

Aristarchus had in fact anticipated the modern theory of the solar system, but it was not only rejected by the ancients, it would be another 1,800 years before Copernicus would establish it once and for all. But well-informed people did begin accepting that the earth was a sphere, especially when the great Greek philosopher Aristotle proved this. Aristotle, who lived from 384 to 322 B.C., also was one of the first to divide the globe into zones. Perhaps his greatest contribution, however, to revealing that there was a world out there waiting to be discovered and explored, was to have tutored a young prince who went on to become Alexander the Great.

True, these early Greek geographers were deskbound men, but some of their work was highly relevant to the discovery and exploration of the world. Perhaps the most notable example of this was the work of Eratosthenes, who became the head of the Alexandrian Library in 247 B.C. Like many such men of that time, he was proficient in various areas—poetry, literary criticism, philosophy, history, mathematics, astronomy, and geography. It was these last three disciplines that he employed to calculate the polar circumference of the Earth with amazing accuracy: Although it is impossible to make an exact conversion of the unit of measurement that he used, it seems he came up with a figure of about 24,662 miles, whereas the measurement, with all the latest technology, is 24,860 miles.

But the importance of Eratosthenes for exploration is not in that simple figure—for one thing, it remained unknown to most people for many centuries. More important was his concept of climate zones, his awareness of the Arctic and Antarctic regions, and the calculation of many of the parallels, or lines of latitude. Of course he was far from correct in many details, just as he was in his calculations of the sizes of the Earth's lands and seas, both known and unknown—after all, he had not the slightest idea that the Western Hemisphere lay between the Pillars of Hercules and India.

The first people known in the Western world to claim that the Earth is a complete sphere were followers of the Greek philosopher and mathematician Pythagoras (about 580–unknown B.C.). In this early 16th-century woodcut, he is shown (on the right) with the late Roman philosopher Boethius (about A.D. 480–524) and a woman probably representing the muse of mathematics. *(Library of Congress, Prints and Photographs Division [LC-USZ62-95297])*

Ephesus, on the coast of southwestern Turkey, was originally an important Greek city; conquered by the Persians, it was taken by Alexander in 334 B.C. and became a major center of the Hellenistic world. Even after the Romans took it over in 133 B.C., it retained its prominence as witnessed by the remains of a temple built by Emperor Hadrian in A.D. 130. *(© Philip Baird www.anthroarcheart.org)*

India; that the summer monsoon season caused great floods; and that a large island, Taprobane (Sri Lanka), lay off India's coast.

Megashenes was not the only Greek who contributed greatly to the knowledge of the world in the Hellenistic Era. There was Agatharchides from Cnidos, a Greek colony on the southwestern tip of Asia Minor (modern Turkey). Born about 140 B.C., he wrote knowledgeably about both the Erythraean Sea (the ancient Greeks' name for what is today the Red Sea, and sometimes also including the Indian Ocean and Persian Gulf) and the lands bordering it, particularly modern Yemen, on the Arabian Peninsula, and Ethiopia, in what was then southern Egypt. For this latter land, Agatharchides gave a full and graphic account of its gold mines, and he spares nothing in describing the slaves forced to work there:

> Unkempt, untended as they are, without even a rag to hide their shame, the awful misery of these sufferers is a spectacle to move the hardest heart. None of them, whether sick or maimed or aged, not even weak women, meet with compassion or respite; all are forced by blows to work without intermission until they expire under this hard treatment, So overpowering is their affliction that they are ever anticipating worse evils in the future and welcome death as a blessed change from life.

It appears that Agatharchides depended on others for his account. Another Greek of the Hellenistic era who definitely did base many of his observations about the Earth on firsthand experiences was Posidonius. Born in Syria about 135 B.C., he was immensely learned and wrote on a variety of subjects, but it was his works on meteorology and the ocean that contributed most to the ancients' knowledge of the earth. Drawing on his extensive travels throughout the Mediterranean region and into France (and possibly as far as Britain), he wrote about the depth of that sea, the role of earthquakes and volcanoes in forming particular features of the landscape, and—most important—the influence of the sun as well as the moon on producing the highest "spring" tides. So influential was Posidonius that, unfortunately, his wrong calculation of the circumference of the Earth was long accepted instead of the correct calculation by Eratosthenes.

By the time Agatharchides and Posidonius were writing, the whole Hellenistic world had been undergoing a profound change for some time. The Greek language and culture was still widely prevalent, but most of the former empire of Alexander was no longer ruled by the descendants of those Macedonians and Greeks who divided up Alexander's empire. Instead, a new power was in control and would gradually displace the Greek culture and language. That power was Rome, and it was about to dominate an empire even larger than Alexander's.

6

THE EXPANSIVE ROMANS

 The Romans who took over Alexander's realm and went on to dominate an empire larger than any up to that time were Latini, members of a large group of people who inhabited west-central Italy. As late as 600 B.C., the Romans were an obscure people living in not much more than an agricultural community (the city of Rome does not even appear in known writings until about 400 B.C.), but in the ensuing 325 years, they gradually extended their power over much of the Italian peninsula. They had accomplished this by military might, to be sure, but they had also succeeded by establishing colonies of Romans throughout Italy, by building roads, by forming political alliances, and by a general tolerance of the cultures of the peoples whom they conquered. By and large, it would be this mix of means that would eventually allow them to extend their empire from the North Atlantic to the Caspian Sea and Persian Gulf.

Yet as successful as they were as empire builders, the Romans were not great explorers in the conventional sense. Their military forces certainly moved into remote lands, they sent out trading expeditions to distant places, they wrote books about both familiar and exotic places, but in the roll call of great explorers—individuals who set forth primarily to discover and investigate—there are virtually no Romans. In fact, for all their boldness in extending the borders of their empire, they never really ventured into the unknown. During the many centuries that the Romans were so dominant, however, they contributed greatly to consolidating what was known about the world.

THE ROMANS EXPAND

Having taken over Italy south of the Alps by 275 B.C., the Romans began to move onto the larger stage of the Mediterranean world. At once, they confronted the major power in the western Mediterranean, the port-city of Carthage, the colony of the Phoenicians who had earlier challenged the Greeks in this region. In what are known as the Punic Wars (the name derived from the Latin for "Phoenician"), which extended intermittently from 264 B.C. to 146 B.C., the Romans not only drove the Carthaginians out of their several colonies in the western Mediterranean—Sicily, Sardinia, Corsica, and above all, Spain—but in

146 B.C. captured and destroyed Carthage itself. Rome now found itself master of the western Mediterranean and a large part of North Africa.

To its north and northeast, Rome faced various challenges. Gallic tribes from France invaded northern Italy but were defeated in 225 B.C. During the ensuing century, Rome asserted its authority over the peoples along the northern frontiers of the Alps and all the way from Portugal and Spain across southern France to the Dalmatian coast, the western shore of the Adriatic Sea.

Meanwhile, Romans had also been battling the remnants of Alexander's Hellenistic empire in the east. By 189 B.C., Rome had defeated Antiochus III, grandson of the Seleucus I who had ruled the empire in Asia, and effectively took control of the coastal lands and islands of the eastern Mediterranean. In 196 B.C., Rome had defeated the Macedonians under Philip V, heir to Alexander's original

This 16th-century engraving depicts the Romans capturing the powerful Phoenician port-city of Carthage on the coast of Africa (present-day Tunisia) in 146 B.C. The Romans then completely destroyed Carthage to prevent the Carthaginians from ever again challenging them. *(Library of Congress, Prints and Photographs Division [LC-USZ62-88804])*

Throughout their conquered lands, the Romans introduced their culture and architecture. The six columns here are all that remain of the grandiose Temple of Jupiter at Baalbek in Lebanon, constructed between A.D. 138 and 217. *(Library of Congress, Prints and Photographs Division [LC-USZ62-106198])*

kingdom that included Greece as well as Macedonia; after subsequent challenges to Rome's authority, Rome simply annexed Macedonia as a province in 147 B.C. The next year—the same year that Rome destroyed Carthage—Rome crushed all resistance in Greece by destroying its great city of Corinth.

During the next 100 years, Rome continued to expand its possessions. Numidia was a kingdom in northwest Africa—roughly today's Algiers—and after a series of wars against its rulers, such as Jugurtha and Juba I, Numidia was reduced to a Roman province after 46 B.C. At the other end of their empire, after a series of wars against Mithridates VI in Asia Minor (mainly today's Turkey) and his suicide in 63 B.C., Rome extended its control over Alexander's old empire in Syria and Asia Minor.

The Romans had assembled their empire in hardly more than 200 years, and they had done so in the face of almost constant resistance by the conquered peoples and internal struggles among various Roman leaders. But there can be no pretending that the Romans who led the victorious forces had much more in mind than exploiting the conquered lands and peoples—plundering their possessions, taxing them, exporting their chief crops and produce, and generally extracting as much as possible. There is little to suggest that Romans had much interest in these new and distant lands. There were no great Roman geographers or historians, let alone explorers or even travelers, during these centuries.

Perhaps the one major exception, Polybius (ca. 203 B.C.–120 B.C.), himself a Greek under the patronage of a powerful Roman general,

After the Romans conquered much of Gaul—modern France—they constructed many public works. Among the most impressive that survive to this day is this aqueduct known as the Pont du Gard, designed to bring water into the Roman city of Nemausus (modern Nîmes) in southern France. It was built during the reign of Augustus (27 B.C.–A.D. 14). *(Library of Congress, Prints and Photographs Division [LC-USZ62-103327])*

traveled throughout parts of Spain, Gaul (France), the Alpine region, and northwestern Africa. His ambitious *Universal History* (part of which survives in the original, part of which is known from later historians), although mostly devoted to Roman military history, does assign one section to the geography of the Mediterranean. Aside from that, and his own travels into little-known parts of Africa—perhaps as far south as the Senegal River—Polybius expressed several views that placed him apart from many ancients. For example, although he focused mostly on historical events, he was constantly describing the geographic features of the settings of these events, because "what men want to know is, not so much the fact that a thing took place as the way in which it happened." And his assertion that traveling to places was important to any historian or geographer—"for the eyes are more accurate witnesses than the ears"—was in effect an endorsement of exploration.

The first Roman who put this into practice was a man who, for all his many achievements, never thought of himself as an explorer: Julius Caesar.

JULIUS CAESAR THE LEADER

Julius Caesar was born into an aristocratic Roman family in 100 B.C. and, like many young

This mid-19th-century engraving is an artist's version of Julius Caesar and his fleet landing on the shore of England in 54 B.C. Although Caesar had landed in England the year before, this was his first ambitious invasion; after several battles, he returned to France. *(Library of Congress, Prints and Photographs Division [LC-USZ62-92891])*

men of his class, went off to Athens to study philosophy and oratory. He next did what youths of his class did, put in some time with the Roman army, first in Asia Minor, then Syria and Spain. When he returned to Rome it was with a burning desire to achieve public office. In 65 B.C. he was placed in charge of Rome's department of the public works and state-sponsored games, and he used this office to gain favor with the masses, much to the annoyance of more conservative Romans. In 62 B.C. Caesar moved up a notch to the position of praetor, a cross between a supreme justice and a military governor—in his case, over Spain. In 59 B.C. he was elected one of the two consuls, the most powerful position in Rome, and not unexpectedly he made the most of his office and once more antagonized many conservatives. A man could only serve as consul in Rome for one year and after that was assigned the right to virtually absolute rule over one of Rome's provinces, including the right to command an army there. Caesar managed to get assigned not only to Cisalpine Gaul—Gaul "this side of the Alps," meaning northern Italy—but also Transalpine Gaul (Gaul beyond the Alps).

In 58 B.C. Caesar moved into Transalpine Gaul, determined to once and for all suppress the many rebellious peoples of Gaul—which included not only France but parts of Belgium, Germany, and Switzerland. Caesar would later write of this vast territory in one of the most famous opening sentences in all literature: *Gallia omnis divisa in partes tres*—"All Gaul is divided into three parts." For the next nine years, Caesar conducted an almost constant series of campaigns and battles, putting down not only the Gauls west of the Rhine River in France but at one point crossing the Rhine—the first Roman general to do so—and pursuing some of the Germanic tribes, just to let them know the power of Rome.

In 55 B.C. he did something even more daring—he led a small force across the Strait of Dover to the island of Britain. This was merely a reconnaissance expedition, and he barely left the coast, spending much of the time repairing their ships damaged in a storm, although the Britons engaged the Romans in two fierce battles. But in 54 B.C. he took a larger force—five legions (the basic Roman infantry unit) and 2,000 cavalry—and this time moved inland, crossing the Thames River some 80 miles from the coast. He met little opposition and at one point captured a prominent British chieftain, Cassivelaunus, but after a few months he returned to Gaul to pursue Rome's enemies there. With his defeat of the Gallic chieftain, Vercingetorix, in 52 B.C., Caesar achieved his greatest victory, and he anticipated that he would be welcomed back to Rome as the conquering hero, but his rivals there had now come to distrust his ambition, and he was told to give up command of his army on January 1, 49 B.C. Instead, Caesar led 5,000 of his most loyal men to the border between his provinces and Roman Italy, the Rubicon River (just north of Rimini, on the coast of northeastern Italy). Hesitating only momentarily, he crossed it, thus inspiring the expression used to this day, "crossing the Rubicon," to describe some irreversible and momentous decision.

From this point on, Caesar's story becomes one of the great dramas of history: his rapid conquest of Italy, his appointment as dictator, his pursuit and conquest of his Roman enemies from Spain to Egypt, his affair with Egyptian queen Cleopatra (who would turn out to be the last of the Ptolemaic Dynasty to rule Egypt), his numerous reforms and populist measures, his attempts to conciliate the conservatives—all swept aside by the strokes of the swords of the men who assassinated him on March 15, 44 B.C. Clearly, Caesar was one of the most energetic, most talented,

In 49 B.C. Julius Caesar led his army across the Rubicon River in northeastern Italy, thus committing himself to challenge the authorities in Rome. This episode is here depicted by an early 19th-century artist. *(Library of Congress, Prints and Photographs Division [LC-USZ62-115312])*

most intelligent, most forceful individuals in all history, but he was also one of the most ambitious, most strong-willed, most manipulative, and most ruthless. He was not greatly cruel or inhuman like certain tyrants—but definitely a man who sought absolute power.

JULIUS CAESAR AND THE HISTORY OF EXPLORATION

Julius Caesar deserves a place in the history of exploration because of one book he wrote: *De*

Bello Gallica (literally "On the Gallic War," but usually referred to as "Commentaries on the Gallic War"). Caesar's own account of the campaigns from 58 through 52 B.C. (a trusted officer, Aulus Hirtius, completed the work through the final campaign of 50 B.C.) is regarded as one of the masterworks of classical literature because of its crystal-clear style and the sheer precision of its observations. Caesar not only described his strategies, tactics, and the actual battles, he wrote of the natural features and peoples of Gaul—and to

All Roads Lead . . .

An old saying states that "All roads lead to Rome." However, Rome was not the first ancient state to build roads—the Persian Empire was famed for its roads—but most of the pre-Roman roads outside cities were not paved. It was the Romans who built the most extensive system of intercity paved roads (although it should be admitted that dirt roads were easier on horses' hooves). The first great Roman road was the Via Appia, begun in 312 B.C. to lead from Rome to Capua (just north of Naples); by 244 B.C. it went to Brindisi on the eastern coast opposite Greece. In 220 B.C. the Romans built the Via Flaminia to lead northeastward to the Adriatic coast; starting in 187 B.C. it was extended northwest to Placentia (modern Piacenza), creating a stretch that became known as the Via Aemilia; eventually it was extended to Genoa as the Via Julia Augusta III. About 130 B.C., Rome built the Via Egnatia, which stretched all the way from the modern Albanian port of Durres (ancient Dyrrhachium) on the Adriatic coast across Macedonia and northern Greece to the great city of Byzantium (later Istanbul). Those were the great roads, but there were many more throughout the empire. And these roads were not just paved on the surface—with either flagstones, gravel, or concrete—they were solidly constructed, often with foundation layers that were four feet deep. High-ranking officials were made responsible for their upkeep, and they did their job so well that many stretches of the Roman highway system remained in use 1,500 years later (and some can be traveled on today). True, they were built to move armed forces quickly to all points of the empire, but they also supported the Romans' postal system. Some official messengers traveled in horse-drawn carriages, others ran on foot; although the average speed has been calculated at 50 miles per day, there are accounts of important messages traveling as fast as 160 miles a day.

a lesser extent, of Britain—in a way that for the first time illuminated them for the Mediterranean peoples. Greek and Roman traders and merchants had been presences in Gaul for centuries, but strangely even the more educated Greeks and Romans seemed to know more about the lands and peoples to their east. Caesar brought Western Europe into the circle of the known.

Caesar eventually visited almost every district of Gaul, a region that the Romans up to then had dismissed as "Hairy Gaul," to express their disdain for its "barbaric" inhabitants.

Caesar, however, described the Gauls with the kind of objectivity that demanded respect. Thus, he turned the Romans' notion of the Gauls' "barbaric" ways inside out when he said of the Belgae, a group of northern Gauls: "They are the most courageous because they are farthest removed from the culture and civilization of [the Romans] and least often visited by merchants introducing the commodities that make for effeminacy." Caesar was one of the first to introduce the Druidic religion to the larger classical world. He wrote:

The Druids are concerned with divine worship, the due performance of sacrifices, public and private, and the interpretation of ritual questions; a great number of young men gather about them for the sake of instruction and hold them in great honor. In fact, it is they who decide in almost all disputes, public or private; and if any crime has been committed or murder done, or there is any dispute about succession or boundaries, they also decide it, determining rewards and penalties. . . . The Druids usually hold aloof from war and do not pay war-taxes with the rest; they are excused from military service and exempt from all liabilities. . . . The cardinal doctrine that they seek to teach is that souls do not die, but after death pass from one to another, and this belief, as the fear of death is thereby cast aside, they hold to be the greatest incentive to valor.

Romans would recognize some aspects of the Druids and perhaps disapprove of others, but they would come away with a new respect for these people.

Above all, Caesar described many basic geographic features of the vast territory, often identifying quite accurately mountains, rivers, coastlines, and plains that had always been the subject of false reports. Of course, he was not always correct in his details. Thus he describes the island of Britain:

A triangular island with one side, about 500 miles long, opposite Gaul; one end of this side, the one in Kent, faces east, the other faces south. The second side, 700 miles long, faces Spain and the west; on this side is Hibernia [Ireland], half as large as Britain, and between them is Mona [Isle of Man]; there are thought to be several other islands where, according to some writers, at the time of the winter solstice, night lasts for thirty days. The third side of Britain, 800 miles long, faces north and there is no land opposite; one end of this side is toward Germany.

Caesar was wrong both about the total length of Britain's "sides" and about the orientation of the island in relation to continental Europe. And he really knew little about the land and people beyond the southeast corner. But the force of his reputation was such that more Romans than ever would become interested in Britain, and eventually Romans would return to conquer much of the island.

AUGUSTUS AND THE PAX ROMANA

Although Rome under Julius Caesar was, for all intents and purposes, an empire, it was not formally declared one until his adopted son and chosen successor, Gaius Julius Caesar Octavianus, became emperor under the name of Augustus in 27 B.C. Augustus continued to expand the boundaries of the Roman Empire, although largely at its fringes—in North Africa, northern Spain, and Asia Minor. Of his two major additions, one was a large strip in Europe that extended Rome's dominion up to the Danube River and included most of what is today Switzerland, southern Germany, Austria, Hungary, the former Yugoslavia, and Bulgaria. The other was Egypt, which he reduced to a Roman province after defeating the fleets of Egypt's queen Cleopatra and her Roman husband, Marc Antony, in 31 B.C. at the famous battle of Actium, off the west coast of Greece.

But Augustus, during his long rule from 44 B.C. to A.D. 14, did something even more important than enlarge the empire. He imposed a relative peace and order by maintaining a disciplined army even at the most remote frontier outposts, assigning responsi-

MAJOR ROMAN ROADS IN ITALY, 312 B.C.–A.D. 14

ble administrative officials, sending out colonies of Romans, developing a postal system, and extending the Roman highway system. The Romans had long recognized the importance of maintaining a good road system, but now they also introduced more exact

After Augustus defeated Cleopatra and Marc Antony in 31 B.C., Egypt was reduced to a Roman province. Symbolizing Rome's dominance is this Roman arch built on top of Egyptian columns at a temple at Biggeh on the Nile. *(Library of Congress, Prints and Photographs Division [LC-USZC4-8558])*

measurements of the distances as well as more precise location of towns. One of the famous works of Augustus's time was the so-called Wall Map of Agrippa. Agrippa was one of Augustus's most faithful subordinates, highly successful both as a military leader and as a civil administrator. He compiled a geographical account of the empire of his day; apparently a large map was based on it and Augustus had this map displayed on a new building, the Porticus Octaviae, named after his sister Octavia. Alongside this great map were the dimensions of Rome's far-flung provinces and the distances between major places. (This map vanished among the ruins of ancient Rome.)

It was the policies of Augustus that commenced the famous *Pax Romana*—the Roman Peace that endured for some 225 years throughout the empire. He himself was an eminently practical man, totally dedicated to preserving the Roman Empire. He would dispatch military expeditions to quell insurrections in or conquer known lands, but he does not seem to have shown any interest in sponsoring expeditions to unknown lands. But Roman soldiers and sailors, merchants and traders, craftsmen and entrepreneurs, spread

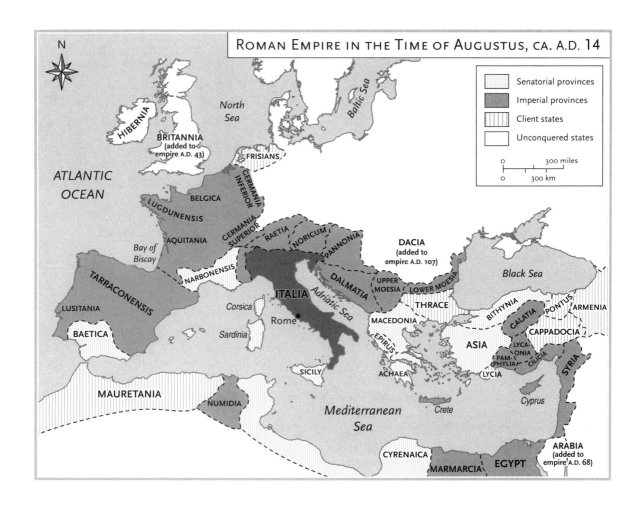

The Romans had conquered much of Britain by the mid-second century A.D., and they set about introducing their culture and structures as they did throughout their empire. Famed for their public baths, this is a view of the one the Romans built over a natural hot spring and which gave its name to the city of Bath, England. *(Library of Congress, Prints and Photographs Division [LC-DIG-ppmsc-07996])*

out through the empire, introducing Roman ways to other peoples and introducing other peoples' ways to Romans. The Pax Romana also created the conditions that encouraged people from all over the vast empire to venture forth. During the reign of Augustus, for example, a man known only as Isadore of Charax—probably somewhere in Persia—traveled overland from the Euphrates River all the way to Afghanistan and described his trip in a work known as the *Parthian Stations* (be-

cause at this time, that territory belonged to a powerful tribe known as the Parthians).

After Augustus died in A.D. 14, he was succeeded by a series of emperors who, in general, left the empire much as it had been under Augustus. One major exception, however, was Rome's gradual conquest of much of Britain, beginning under Claudius, who ruled from A.D. 41–54. During the next 100 years the Romans extended their rule over Britain to the narrow strip of land that lies just north of

Edinburgh and Glasgow, Scotland, and in the course of the almost 400 years that they dominated Britain, the Romans gained considerable knowledge of that land. At the other extreme of the empire, the Emperor Trajan (ruling from A.D. 98–117) annexed a region known as Dacia (which included most of modern Romania and a part of Hungary) and brought under firm Roman control Armenia and Mesopotamia, which had fallen prey to foreign tribesmen in the years since the disintegration of Alexander's empire.

In fact, one way to look at Rome's empire was that it simply reassembled the pieces of Alexander's shattered empire, added several more, and then advanced even further the cosmopolitan spirit that had commenced in the Hellenistic Age, as peoples from all over the Roman Empire regarded themselves as citizens of this new world. And if there are no major discoveries or great individual explorers during this period, there were numerous writings that advanced the knowledge of this great empire. Often the authors were writing primarily to describe and glorify the Roman military conquests, but these accounts also included a great deal of geographic detail.

Theophanes, for example, was a Greek of the first century B.C. from the Roman-controlled island of Mitilini, off the northeastern coast of Asia Minor. He provided quite a detailed description of the Caucasus, the mountainous region between the Black and Caspian Seas (now shared by Russia, Georgia, Armenia, and Azerbaijan). Theophanes not only described features of its landscape but also provided much new information about the inhabitants of the Caucasus. Or there was Pomponius Mela, a Roman from Spain, who in the first century A.D. wrote a geographical survey of what he knew of the inhabited world. There was little original in this work— he subscribed to the prevailing view of the

time that there were only three continents (Europe, Asia, and Africa) surrounded by one ocean. But he did provide some details about the physical features, climate, and customs of the lands.

The two great historians/geographers of this era, however, were Strabo (63 B.C.–A.D. 21), a Greek by descent, and Pliny the Elder (A.D. 23–A.D. 79). Although Strabo seems to have done some traveling simply to inform himself, Pliny seems to have traveled primarily on military or governmental assignments. But it is to their writings that future generations owe a great

Strabo (63 B.C.–A.D. 21), of Greek descent, traveled widely throughout the Roman Empire. His *Geography* both surveyed much of the world known to Europeans and incorporated many of the only surviving accounts of early explorers. In this 16th-century engraving, he is shown holding the world globe. *(Library of Congress, Prints and Photographs Division [LC-USZ62-99999])*

A Roman Road Map

One of the most extraordinary documents from the ancient world is the so-called Peutinger Table. This was essentially a road map for much of what Romans knew of the world of the late third century A.D. Who was responsible for it is unknown, and the original was lost, but it was copied in the 13th century by a German monk. That copy was lost until it surfaced in the 16th century, thanks to a German scholar, Konrad Peutinger. It is in the form of a long strip—some 21 feet long and one foot high—divided into 12 sections so it could be folded, much like a road map today. The continuous map extends from the southwestern corner of Britain to the mouth of the Ganges River, in the eastern corner of India; the distances are greatly elongated, and only major roads, towns, rivers, and mountains are indicated. Whoever made it was not interested in accurately portraying the shape of geographic features but in showing the main route. It even uses symbols much as modern maps do—a house for a small town, wall and towers for large towns, a bathhouse tank for watering places. Clearly, it was one of a kind and very likely was made for some official use, but it communicates like an amazingly recognizable voice from the past.

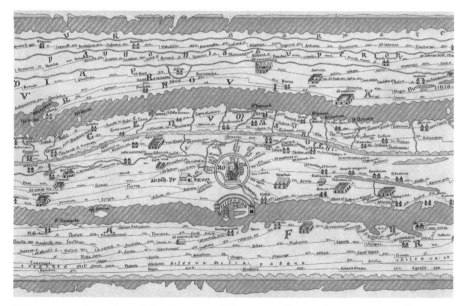

This is a small section of the Peutinger Table, a road map that was originally drawn for the Romans of the late third century A.D. The section here shows central Italy, with Rome at the center and a network of roads that lead to adjacent countries. *(from* Classical Atlas, *by Alexander G. Findlay. New York: Harper and Brothers, 1849; print courtesy of The General Libraries, The University of Texas at Austin)*

deal about not only their contemporaries' ideas of the world but also of previous accounts of the world by earlier explorers. Strabo's *Geography* was a major survey of the world, all the way from India in the east to the Scilly Islands off Britain's southwesternmost coast, and from northern Europe to Ethiopia in Africa. He was by no means "scientific," but he is the sole source of many of the earlier accounts of explorations.

The same can be said of Pliny the Elder (A.D. 23–A.D. 79), who combined a career in the military with that of a writer. Of his many volumes, only one work survives, the *Naturalis Historia,* which drew from hundreds of other authors to present an encyclopedia of natural history—geography, zoology, botany, mineralogy, anthropology, pharmacology, and more. In so doing, Pliny preserved many excerpts from older writers that would have otherwise been totally lost. Pliny was by no means an original scientist, but he was a curious man, and his curiosity led to his death: When he saw that the volcano Vesuvius was erupting in August 79, he sailed to the nearby coast to get a closer look and was asphyxiated by the poisonous atmosphere.

ROME AND THE EAST

As indicated before, the Romans took great care of and interest in their own empire but they did not show much interest in reaching out beyond its borders, preferring instead to leave that to middlemen. Greeks, especially, were left to deal with peoples to the east. Sometime in the early part of the first century A.D., for example, a Greek merchant of whom nothing is known except his name, Hippalus, is said to have become familiar with the lands bordering the Arabian Sea and also with the seasons' prevailing winds of that area. One summer he put his knowledge to the test and sailed quite easily from the tip of the Arabian Peninsula to the mouth of the Indus River; then in the winter, when the wind direction changed, he returned from India to Arabia. After several such voyages, word of this strategy spread and helped to increase trade between the Roman Empire and India.

Hippalus and his achievement are known only from another anonymous Greek's work, the *Periplus Maris Erythraei,* or "Sailing around the Erythraean Sea," a navigator's guide to the coasts of the lands that border the Arabian Sea and Indian Ocean—Africa, Arabia, and India. Dated to somewhere between A.D. 50 and 90, it is a remarkable document, detailing not only the natural features of the coasts but also the main ports and trading stations and their exports and imports. It was clearly a guide for merchants, but it also included a great deal of basic geographical information, as exemplified by this description of the extremely strong tidal flow of the Mahi River along the west central coast of India:

> So great indeed is the violence with which the sea comes in at the new moon, especially during the nightly flow of the tide, that, while at the commencement of its advance, when the sea is calm, a sound like the shouting of an army far away reaches the ears of those who dwell about the estuary, and shortly afterwards the sea itself with a rushing noise comes sweeping over the shallows.

This Periplus, however, is notable for another feature. Although the author of the coastal guide seems to have firsthand knowledge only down to about 500 miles northwest of the tip of the Indian peninsula, he mentions reports of points much farther on—not only along the eastern coast of India but even eastward to what was most likely the peninsula of

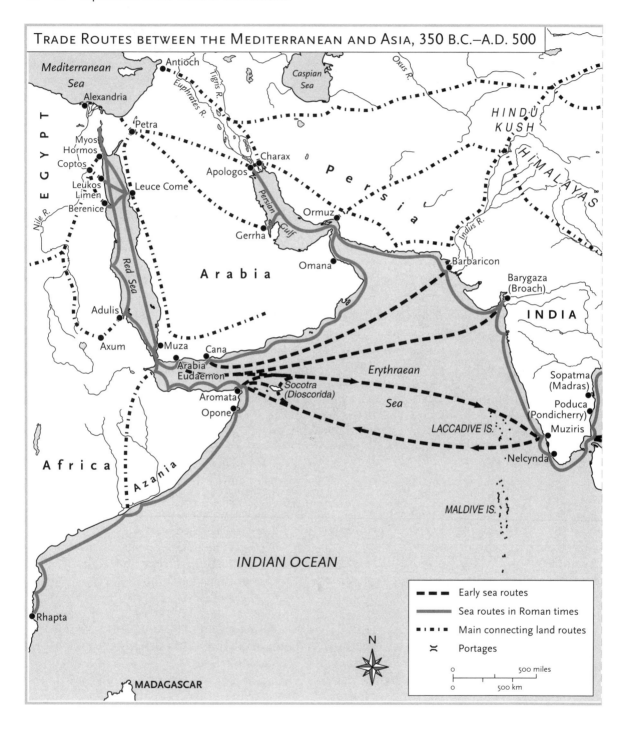

TRADE ROUTES BETWEEN THE MEDITERRANEAN AND ASIA, 350 B.C.–A.D. 500

- - - Early sea routes
━━━ Sea routes in Roman times
·-·-·- Main connecting land routes
≻≺ Portages

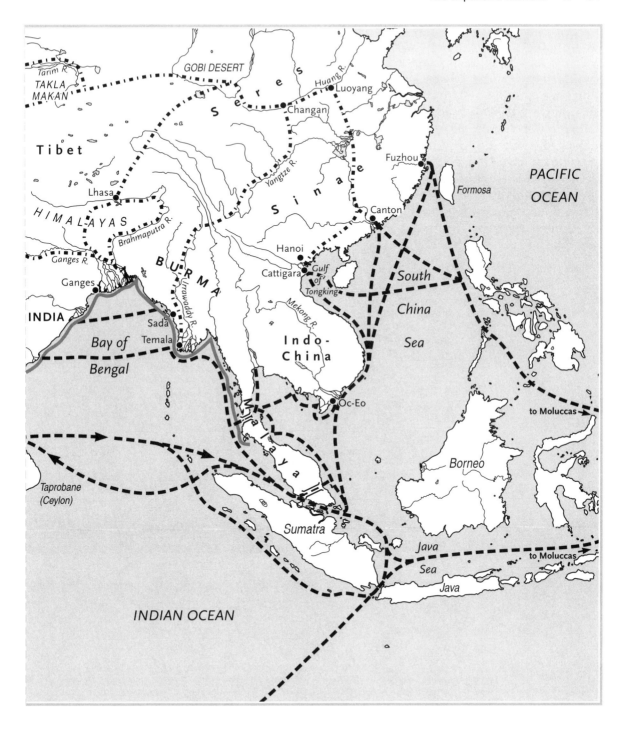

Malay, and still farther. He reports a distant land where "there is a great inland city called Thina, from which raw silk and silk yarn and silk cloth are brought overland." Although scholars cannot agree on exactly what city he was referring to, they tend to agree that the people producing the silk were Chinese, thus making this one of the earliest references to the Chinese in Western accounts.

Silk itself was by no means an unknown product in the West at this time—late first century A.D.—at least in Rome. In the first century B.C., Roman historians reported, silk was used to make awnings for Julius Caesar's ceremonies and for Cleopatra's dresses. Clearly, though, it was a luxury reserved for the most powerful. Just as clearly, even the Romans who knew about silk remained uncertain about its source as they obtained it through middlemen at the fringes of their empire. It would not be long, though, before Rome would deal directly with China and Asia and discover a continent with its own distinguished history and attainments in the field of exploration.

7

CHINA'S AND ASIA'S ROLE IN EXPLORATION

 By the time of the reign of Augustus (27 B.C.–A.D. 14), the Mediterranean—especially its capital, Rome—did appear to be the hub of the earth. Not only did all roads—and sea routes—lead there, the produce of the world was transported there. This included the basics such as grains and olive oil as well as luxury items, everything from incense and ivory to precious stones and silk. Meanwhile, the troops and administrators of Rome's empire were stationed from the Atlantic to the Nile. It thus seems to make sense to trace the story of discovery and exploration as radiating out from there. But the fact is, peoples in other parts of the world had long been experiencing their own history. Many of these peoples did not have writing systems, so there is little or no record of the many anonymous individuals who ventured forth into distant parts—merchants, mariners, hunters, traders, adventurers, scientists, and just plain curious travelers. But one people in particular can boast of a history as well documented, as far-reaching, and as

distinguished as any in the West. They are the Chinese.

CHINA'S EARLY PHASE

Human beings, modern *Homo sapiens,* appeared in China as early as any place in the world—about 50,000 B.C.—but China's traditional history does not begin until about 2800 B.C. Even the first thousand or so years involved semilegendary individuals and events. It was not until the Shang dynasty (ca. 1750–1040 B.C.) that historians begin to accept a relatively authentic version of events—as usual, because a written language had by then appeared. For some 1,500 years, however—from 1750 to 221 B.C.—China remained a land in almost constant turmoil, by no means a unified nation and certainly not one that embraced all the territory of modern China.

Even by this time, China had its own tradition of geographical writings. The oldest of these texts that has survived, the *Shujing (Shu Ching)* (Historical classic) is believed to

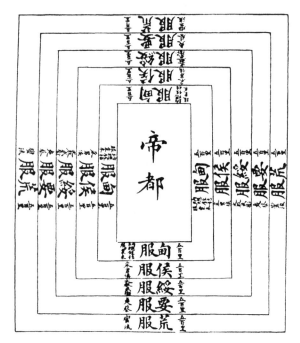

This map is based on text in the *Shujing (Shu Ching); Book of History* (dated to about the fifth century B.C.) and reflects the ancient Chinese view of the world. At the center is the land of the emperor, and successive areas represent the lands of peoples the Chinese regarded as less and less civilized, until the last band represents the area of cultureless savages. *(Library of Congress)*

date to the fifth century B.C.—that is, about 450 B.C., the same time of the great Greek historian/geographer Herodotus. Although it includes references to a legendary Emperor Yu, said to have ruled about 2200 B.C., the *Shu Ching* is basically a survey of the land and resources of China and sounds much like a textbook:

> Between the Chi river and the Yellow River is the province of Yen (the second province). The nine branches of the Yellow River were led into their proper channels. The Lei-hsia district was made into a marsh, and the Yung and Chu rivers joined it. The mulberry grounds were stocked with silkworms, and the people descended from the hills and dwelt in the plains. The soil of this province is black and fat, its grass is luxuriant and its trees are tall.

The point is that these early Chinese took a scientific interest in describing their world. In its systematic detailing of geographic features, in fact the *Shu Ching* was more advanced than any comparable text in the West.

Another well-known book from this era is the *Shan Hai Ching* (Classic of the mountains and rivers). Its contents appear to date from several periods, extending from at least 300 B.C. to as late as A.D. 200. Although it does contain a fair amount of detailed geographical information, this is combined with legend and myth and fantasy—winged men, dog-faced men, bodies with no heads, heads that fly about alone. There are similar tales in Herodotus, but whereas Herodotus's travels can be traced along known routes, the journey described in the *Shan Hai Ching* is regarded by scholars as purely imaginary:

> [I] have walked about three hundred li [1 li = approx. 1/3 of a mile] since Bald Mountain. Here, Bamboo Mountain is near the river that looks like a boundary. There is no grass or trees but some jasper and jade stones. . . . three hundred li to the south, Bald Mountain is found . . . wild animals are found here that look like suckling pigs, but they have pearls. . . . Three hundred li farther south, Bamboo Mountain is found, bordering on a river. . . . There is no grass or trees but there are many green-jasper and green-jade stones.

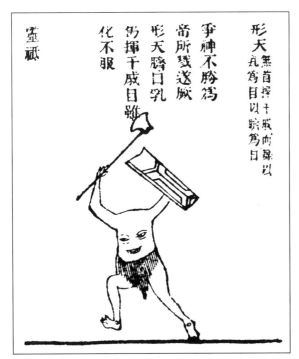

Ancient Chinese geography texts often carried reports and illustrations of fabulous creatures. An example of one such is this headless creature described in the *Chan Haijing* (*Shan Hai Ching*; Classic of the mountains and rivers), a Chinese text dating from between 300 B.C. and A.D. 200. Clearly, this is an imaginary creature, so the issue scholars debate is whether the Chinese had been influenced by tales of similar creatures in earlier European accounts, such as those of Herodotus. *(From Shan Hai Ching, antique géographie chinoise. Paris: J. Maissoneuve, 1891)*

THE HISTORIC PERIOD

The Qin (Ch'in) dynasty that ruled China from 221 to 206 B.C. was the first to impose a certain unity, and it did so in part by building highways and waterways to enable better communication. It was the Qin dynasty that also commenced building the Great Wall along China's northern border to hold back marauding tribes.

The Qin dynasty was soon replaced by the Han dynasty (202 B.C.–A.D. 220), generally rec-

A person similar to the headless creature depicted in the ancient Chinese text (opposite) was described in the work of the Roman geographer, Gaius Julius Solinus, who lived in the third century A.D. Solinus was mainly a collector and repeater of stories widely known throughout the Mediterranean, and it is possible that some of these did get passed on via contacts in the Middle East to Central Asians and then to the Chinese. Some scholars believe that the Chinese were influenced by the European texts. *(From* Polyhistor, The Worthie Work of Iulius Solinus. *London: I. Charleswood for Thomas Hacket, 1587)*

There are people today who claim that the description of this journey fits the landscape and natural resources of parts of the United States—in particular western Texas. Thus the pig with "pearls" is said to be the collared peccary, found in the southwestern United States. Serious scholars, however, reject any such claims.

ognized as providing the foundations of modern China. By the time Wudi assumed the throne in 141 B.C., the Han had established a strong central government, and during his 54-year reign he expanded the dynasty's power in all directions—including into Korea. In particular, Wudi (Wu-ti) wanted to know more about the Yuezhi peoples far to the west, with the goal of perhaps making an alliance with them against the Xiongnu, a people who lived to the northwest of Han China (today's Mongolia). In 139 B.C. he commissioned Zhang Qian (transliterated also as Chang Chien), a court official, to go on an expedition to the farthest western reaches of China and even into Central Asia.

Zhang Qian proceeded west but was soon captured by the Xiongnu (Hsiung-nu). They held Zhang Qian captive for 10 years—he even married one of their women and had a son with her—but eventually he was able to escape. He continued making his way west to

Pre-Columbian Asians in the Americas?

As it happens, there are a group of reputable scholars who believe that some Chinese and other Asians may have made their way to the Americas many centuries before Columbus. These scholars believe that at four different points of time, at least small numbers of Asians arrived on the shores of Middle or South America on rafts or small boats that drifted or were blown across the Pacific. According to these scholars, the first of these trans-Pacific contacts occurred about 300 B.C. when some Japanese landed in Ecuador; the scholars cite as evidence the type of pottery that appeared there at this time in Ecuador and was made with techniques and designs very similar to Japanese pottery of that time. The second contact occurred sometime between 1000 and 500 B.C., and this time it was Chinese who landed in Mexico; according to the scholars, these Chinese introduced into the Olmec Indian culture various elements such as jade carving and mirrors as ritual objects. The third period came about the beginning of what became known as the Christian Era; it involved more Chinese who came into Mexico and some Southeast Asians who came into Peru. The fourth period then occurred between about A.D. 500 and 700 when more Southeast Asians made contact with the Maya of Central America.

The evidence for these last two periods of contact, according to the scholars, is found in such cultural influences as the introduction of metalwork, types of pottery, certain architectural details, the use of ritual objects, and above all in artistic motifs in sculpture and paintings. Most authorities on this phase of history of the Americas do not accept the claims of "trans-Pacific contacts," as this theory is known. Admittedly, there is a thin line separating the claims of these scholars and the claims made by so many who find pre-Columbian traces of virtually every people in the world. There is a claim, for example, that black Africans got to the Americas before Columbus; the main

a region today belonging to Uzbekistan and Kyrgysztan. He was unable to persuade the people there to join the Han against the Xiongnu, so after about a year with them he headed back. Once again, he was captured by the Xiongnu, but this time he escaped after only about a year and made his way back to the capital, Chang'an.

Emperor Wudi rewarded Zhang Qian with the post of a palace counselor. Although he had failed to enlist allies against the Xiongnu, he brought back a great deal of information about this region, including an account of a larger breed of horses than the Chinese had available. He also brought back samples of at least three natural products unknown to the Chinese—grapes, walnuts, and pomegranates. (Not long after his return, the Chinese began to use the grape design on the backs of mirrors.) If Zhang Qian wrote an account of his adventure, it did not survive; everything that is known about him comes from one of

proponent, a professor Ivan Van Sertima, relies on much the same kind of evidence as do the "trans-Pacific" proponents. About all that most people can do when it comes to pre-Columbian contacts is to keep an open mind but examine all sides carefully.

The Chinese early developed a distinctive ship—flat-bottomed, with a high stern and sails extended with strips of wood—that is known as a junk (based on the Javanese word for these ships). The junk pictured here from the early 20th century probably does not differ that much from ships sailed by the Chinese for thousands of years. *(Library of Congress, Prints and Photographs Division [LC-USZ62-91255])*

the most famous works of Chinese History, *Records of the Grand Historian,* by Zhang Qian's near-contemporary, Sima Qian (Ssu-ma Chien) (ca. 145–90 B.C.), the most authoritative account of the lands to the west that the Chinese would have for some time:

> Anxi [Persia] is located several thousand li west of the region of the Yuezhi's land. The people live on the land, cultivating the fields and growing rice and wheat. They also make wine out of grapes. They have walled cities. . . . the region contains several hundred cities of various sizes. . . . The coins of the country are made of silver and bear the face of the king, When the king dies, the currency is immediately changed and new coins are issued with the face of his successor. . . . Tiaozhi {Mesopotamia] is situated several thousand li west of Anxi and borders the Western Sea [Persian Gulf]. It is hot and damp, and the people live by cultivating the fields and planting rice . . . When I was in Daxia [Bactria, now northern Afghanistan], I saw bamboo canes from Qiong [a Chinese region] and cloth made in the province of Shu [another Chinese region]. When I asked people how they had gotten such articles, they replied, "Our merchants go to buy them in the markets of Shendu [India]." Shendu, they tell me, lies several thousand li southwest of Daxia. The people cultivate the land and live much like the people of Daxia. The region is said to be hot and damp. The inhabitants ride elephants when they go into battle. The kingdom is situated on a great river.

Zhang Qian's description of these lands and their inhabitants aroused the interest of Wudi, and about 125 B.C. he commissioned Zhang Qian to lead a second expedition to Daxia. This expedition was divided into four

groups in an attempt to find the best way through hostile peoples. None of the groups managed to get as far as Zhang Qian had reached on his first expedition. Some did manage, however, to bring back a number of the larger horses that were quickly adopted by the Han cavalry.

THE SILK ROAD

But something even more important came out of Zhang Qian's journeys and report. The Chinese began to send caravans carrying goods overland to the west, in this way avoiding the circuitous sea route through southeast Asia and then the middlemen in India. Soon there developed what has come to be known as the "silk road"—the route from eastern China across its western reaches into Central Asia, and from there across the Middle East to the Mediterranean. That name is slightly misleading. (In fact, it was a name not applied until the 19th century, and then by a German scholar, Baron Ferdinand von Richthofen.) For one thing, there was no single road—there were at least two major roads across China, one a northern route, one the southern route, and several branches off these two routes. But all roads tended to meet at Kashgar, today known as Kashi (or K'oh-shih), in the farthest west of China and still a major commercial center for all Central Asia. There different routes west were possible. One led to Samarkand and along the south of the Caspian Sea; another reached the Caspian Sea via Tashkent; still another went down across the Karakorum into India.

The Chinese and other Asians who conducted these caravans—composed of horses, mules, camels, wagons—did not go all the way to the West. At any point from Kashgar on, traders from other nations than China would

This is an early 20th-century artist's painting of a caravan of camels resting outside the walls of Beijing, and it can be assumed that this is a common scene during the centuries that such caravans carried goods back and forth along the Silk Road. *(Library of Congress, Prints and Photographs Division [LC-USZ62-133695])*

most likely take over the produce and even those merchants would probably turn over the goods to at least one more middleman before it reached the destinations along the Mediterranean Sea and Western Europe. Certainly there were no Chinese seen around the ancient Mediterranean world, any more than there were Romans seen in China until perhaps the late second century A.D.

Another reason the name Silk Road is misleading is that silk was by no means the sole commodity that was transported and traded along this route. Caravans coming from China to the west also carried spices, other textiles,

furs, ceramics, lacquerware, jade, bronze objects, even iron objects, exotic plants, and animals. Meanwhile, caravans heading east from the West carried ivory, gold, precious stones, and glass (one of the few technologies where the West was ahead of the Chinese). Also, along the road, goods were exchanged—often more than once—so that not all the goods that finally reached one end of the route had started out at the other end.

It is also true that Chinese silk was known to some in the West even before Zhang Qian's expedition. This reached the Mediterranean in small quantities and by the efforts of individual traders. It most likely came via India, from where it was traded up through the Persian Gulf and then overland to the shores of the Mediterranean. Sometimes, though, it is claimed that the Romans first saw silk when they were conducting a campaign against the Parthians who lived in Persia (Iran)—this was about 53 B.C. Certainly it was about this time that the Romans began to refer to the "Seres"—the Silk People. And it was from this point on that silk, with its soft texture and attractive colors and designs, became highly popular among the wealthy elite of Rome. The Romans soon began to send out agents to

explore the route by which silk and the other exotic wares were coming to them.

What began as indirect contacts through trade soon led to more direct contacts between the Chinese and Westerners. A famous history of China, composed by Fan Ye about A.D. 435, had a "Chapter on the Western Regions" that discussed China's relations with the Arab world of about A.D. 25–55, describing the people of northern Saudi Arabia and Jordan. Between A.D. 92–102, Ban Chao (Pan Ch'ao), the protector-general of the Silk Road, while suppressing threats from people along the road, went almost to the Caspian Sea and

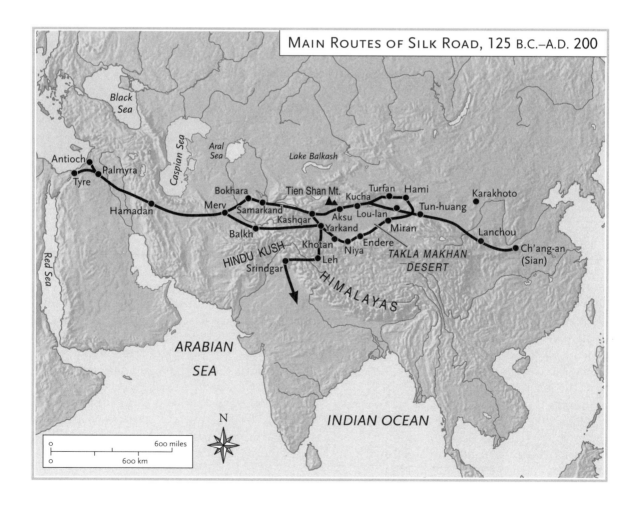

MAIN ROUTES OF SILK ROAD, 125 B.C.–A.D. 200

returned with information about the Romans to the west. Gan Ying (Kan Ying), a Chinese envoy who traveled all the way to Antioch, Syria, about A.D. 97, wrote an account of the people living there, at that time a province of Rome; among other things, he reported that "the people there are honest in their transactions and do not double their prices." Then, in A.D. 166, another Chinese account tells of how during the reign of Emperor Huandi (Huan-ti), "the king of Ta-ts'-in, Antun sent an embassy that, from the frontier of Jih-nan [Annam, or central Vietnam], offered ivory, rhinoceros horns, and tortoise shell." Ta-ts'-in was the Chinese name for the Roman Empire, and Antun is "Antoninus," the family name of the Roman emperor at this time, Marcus Aurelius (A.D. 161–180). What is interesting is that none of these products came from Rome itself, and so they were not all that exotic to the Chinese. In any case, the Chinese report continued, "From that time dates our intercourse with this country."

In fact, by the reign of Marcus Aurelius there were many links between the Mediterranean and Asia—primarily because of the Chinese and Romans, but often as not through middlemen and intermediary countries. India especially provided an alternative route from the Silk Road and served as an intermediary for trade goods. In fact, it is known that as far back as 3000 B.C., traders from the Indus Valley in northern India were trading in Mesopotamia. Trade and knowledge of the world outside India expanded over the centuries; by the early centuries A.D., Indian envoys began to visit the courts of Roman emperors starting with Augustus himself and were also maintaining contacts with Southeast Asia. By A.D. 400, the *Puranas,* a collection of texts revered by the Hindus, contained references to places in Afghanistan, Persia, Russia (including Siberia), China, east-

ern and northern Africa, and even southern Europe.

So Roman or other European merchants did not need to travel to Asia. They could count on caravans making their way overland between the Mediterranean and China or on the sailors and traders who lived along the Persian Gulf and Arabian Sea and Indian Ocean to bring these goods up to the shores of Egypt or Arabia. (Roman coins from this period have been found at places all along this route and even as far east as Cambodia, almost certainly carried to such distances by non-Romans.) Likewise, the Chinese could count on obtaining wares from Africa, India, and the Middle East from middlemen in Central Asia or Southeast Asia. Mariners and merchants moved all along the coasts of India, Malaysia, the Indochina peninsula, and the East Indies islands, exchanging the wares of China and Europe. As a result, there were no known explorers making their way between Europe and Asia during this period.

ON THE TRAIL OF BUDDHISM

One thing that was making its way to China, however, was the Buddhist religion from India. By about A.D. 65, a half brother of Emperor Mingdi (Ming-ti) of China adopted Buddhism, and Buddhists were tolerated in the capital. A later Chinese work claims that Mingdi, having seen the Buddha in a dream, sent envoys to India to learn about his teachings; the envoys returned about the year 67, bringing not only Buddhist texts and statues but two Buddhist monks who started translating the Buddhist writings into Chinese. This may be only a legend, but in the year 166, the cult of Buddha was formally recognized at the imperial court. In 170 Lokakshema, a Bud-

Buddhism across Asia ⌒

The religion of Buddhism had been founded in India about 500 B.C. by Siddhartha Gautama, who came to be known as Buddha, "the Enlightened One." Its basic tenet was that human existence was a continual cycle of death and rebirth and that the way to escape from this was to eliminate attachment to earthly things and so to achieve nirvana, perfect peace and happiness. Beyond shunning the desire for material possessions, Buddhism asked its adherents to respect all forms of life, to free their mind from evil, to control their feelings and thoughts,

and to practice concentration of mind and body. What might seem curious at first glance is that the Buddhist religion, which appears to call for a rather passive approach to the world, spread so rapidly all the way to China. Yet

This sculpture depicting a Dhyani, or meditative adherent of Buddhism, in a typical attitude is at Taxila, an ancient center of Buddhist studies in what is now northeastern Pakistan. Pakistan was then a part of northeastern India, the region where Buddhism first took hold. *(Library of Congress, Prints and Photographs Division [LC-USZ62-116439])*

dhist monk from the region of northern India and Central Asia, arrived in China and formed a team that began to translate some of the Buddhist texts. Within 25 years, large Buddhist communities were flourishing in eastern China.

With the end of the Han dynasty in A.D. 220, China entered into a long period of unrest. Along the Silk Road, trading traffic declined somewhat because the Chinese were not able to maintain order. In China itself, Buddhism spread among the masses because it offered consolation during a time of earthly sufferings, and many Chinese Buddhists made pilgrimages to India, much as Christians would later travel to Jerusalem or Mus-

Buddhism did not arrive in Japan until about A.D. 535, but it spread quickly and by the end of the century was accepted as an official religion. This large (42-foot-high) bronze statue of Buddha is at Kamakura, in Japan, which became a center of Buddhism in the 13th century. *(Library of Congress, Prints and Photographs Division [LC-USZ62-95822])*

the true believers in Buddhism, mostly monks who devoted their entire existence to their faith, were active in promoting their faith by their presence and their writings. So Buddhism spread relatively quickly from India into neighboring lands such as Nepal, Indonesia, Burma, and Sri Lanka. By the first century A.D., foreign converts were introducing Buddhism to the peoples living along the Silk Road, and from there it began to attract Chinese. Buddhism did not always find it easy going in China, which had its "homegrown" faiths, Confucianism and Taoism, and these would eventually contribute to creating a particularly Chinese variety of Buddhism. In the course of moving into China, Buddhism also drew many Chinese to explore the world beyond their own land's boundaries. By the mid-sixth century, Buddhism had spread to Japan.

lims to Mecca. In the year 399, however, a 65-year-old Chinese Buddhist, Faxien (Fa-Hsien), accompanied by several other Buddhist monks, set off for India expressly to obtain some of the sacred Buddhist texts. He walked across central China, across the Taklamakan Desert in far western China, then across Tajikistan and into India, reaching Tamluk (near modern Calcutta), a stronghold of Buddhism. The trip had taken several years, and he spent several more in India before boarding a ship for home. He spent three more years on his trip, sailing by way of Sri Lanka and across the Indian Ocean to Sumatra, then north through the China Sea, arriving home in northern China in 413.

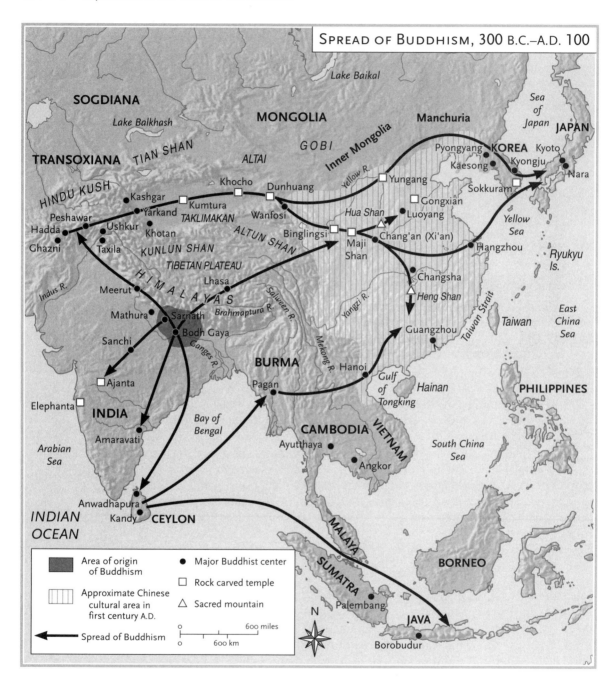

SPREAD OF BUDDHISM, 300 B.C.–A.D. 100

Faxien carried back with him Buddhist texts and images, but more important, he carried his notes and memories of his travels.

These he set down in 414 as the *Record of Buddhist Countries* (more widely known today as *Travels of Faxien*). This work was not just a report of the geographic features of the lands seen during his journey but also a carefully observed account of the history and customs of the peoples he passed through in Central Asia and India, especially of the role of Buddhism in their lives. Thus he says of Yu-teen (Khotan, modern Hotien [Ho-t'ien], in far western China):

> Yu-teen is a pleasant and prosperous kingdom, with a numerous and flourishing population. The inhabitants all profess our Law [that is, Buddhism] and join together in its religious music for their enjoyment. The monks amount to several thousand, most of whom are students of the Mahayana [one of the major branches of Buddhism]. They all receive their food from the common store. Throughout the country the houses of the people stand apart like stars, and each family has a small stupa [a small Buddhist shrine] erected in front of its door. . . . In the monasteries they provide rooms for monks traveling from all quarters and who are provided with whatever else they require.

But he remained a man of his time in his mixture of careful science and mythology, as seen in his description of the Pamir Mountains in Tajikistan:

> The Pamirs are covered with snow both winter and summer. They are inhabited by poisonous dragons. If one arouses the ill humor of the dragons, they will at once call forth poisonous winds, cause snows to fall, or send showers of sand, gravel, and stone flying. Of the persons who have encountered such difficulties, hardly one in ten thousand has escaped without injury.

Whatever his limitations, Faxien was one of the most adventurous travelers of his time, and by his example and his writings he helped

to inspire even more Chinese to travel to India. This increased traffic between India and China contributed not only to opening up these two vast countries but also many other lands between and around them.

By this time—the fifth century A.D.—the Chinese had begun to compile quite an impressive number of texts on geography, some of them dealing with foreign lands on their borders. They were also showing a great interest in making maps. At the same time, there was still a tradition of mixing the fabulous with the real. One of the more curious stories from China's history is said to have been recorded in the *Liang-shu* (Records of the Liang dynasty), an account of the dynasty that briefly ruled southern China in 502–557. The story tells of a Buddhist priest, Hwui Shan (Hsuan-Chuang), who in 499 arrived at the court of the Liang king. He claimed that he had just come from a kingdom he called Fu-sang, which lay far to the east of China—that is, way off across the Pacific Ocean. His account of this place went on as follows:

> It produces many fu-sang trees from which it derives its name. . . . Its fruit resembles the pear, but is red; the bark is spun into cloth for dresses and woven into brocade. The houses are made of planks. There are no walled cities with gates. The people use characters for writing, making paper from the bark of the fu-sang. There are no soldiers wearing metal armor for they do not carry on war.

Hwui Shan went on to describe much else about Fu-sang—its criminal justice system, the ruler's clothing, social classes in great detail, wedding and burial customs. He also claimed that the people of Fu-sang had not known of Buddhism until the year 458, when five Buddhist priests had visited them and tried to convert them.

This was difficult enough to relate to any known land or historical episode. But along with Hwui Shan's account, there were tales of places that seemed to be part of or nearby Fu-sang. One was called the "Kingdom of Women," where there was a "black canyon," a "smoking mountain," a "sea of varnish," and a "sea the color of milk." Here, too, the people lived in round houses, some men had dog heads, and some women married snakes. Most scholars consider these things along with the whole story of Fu-sang as sheer fiction, a story in the age-old and universal tradition of fabulous places. But that has not stopped many people from insisting that all this proves that the Chinese got to the Americas at this time. They locate Fu-sang and the Kingdom of Women in places from British Columbia to Mexico and find analogies in Native American cultures. Thus the fu-sang tree is said to be anything from the prickly pear to the agave plant, known in Mexico as the maguey. The "black canyon" is today said to be the Black Canyon of the Gunnison National Monument in west-central Colorado; the "smoking mountain" is the still-active Volcán de Colima in Mexico; the "sea of varnish" is the La Brea Tar Pits near Los Angeles; the sea "the color of milk" could be one of several dried-up salt-bed lakes in California; the round houses are the adobe houses of the Navajo or Pueblo Indians of the American Southwest; the men with dog heads referred to the masks worn by the Hopi in their Kachina ceremonies; and the women who married snakes referred to a Hopi legend of

The *maguey* of Spanish-speaking Middle Americans (*agave* or *century plant* to North Americans) is claimed to be the fu-sang tree by those who insist that Fu-sang was actually America. It is cultivated for its fiber and sap, but it does not otherwise fit the description of the fu-sang tree. The farm shown here was in El Salvador in the early 20th century. *(Library of Congress, Prints and Photographs Division [LC-USZ62-97811])*

the origin of their Snake Clan. Scholars demand more evidence than such possible similarities, but this has not stopped some people from believing that Chinese got to America by about A.D. 500.

Interestingly, it is mostly Westerners, not Chinese, who have chosen to promote this theory. Long ago, the Chinese came to call their country *Chung-kuo,* which means "Middle Kingdom," indicative of their sense of China as the geographical center of the world and the true center of civilization. For all their careful work in the fields of geography and mapmaking, they saw little need to go forth and explore the world. Instead, they withdrew behind their borders and expected the world to come to them.

8

A WORLD CLOSES IN

By the second century A.D., great changes had taken place in the world since the first civilizations emerged in both the Middle East and Asia some 3,000 years earlier. New lands had been discovered and explored and settled, kingdoms and dynasties and empires had come and gone. Now the world was divided into several main power centers: The Roman Empire dominated from Western Europe across to the Middle East; China dominated from its homeland well across into Central Asia and down into parts of Southeast Asia; India, although in constant turmoil, played the central role in South Asia. Due to the exertions of mariners and merchants, envoys and missionaries, travelers and adventurers, these regions were aware of one another's existence, even if much of the knowledge was sketchy and false. Most especially, there were still large gaps in even the most informed people's knowledge of what composed the entire earth.

PTOLEMY'S WORLD

One of the major centers of the world in the second century A.D., outranked in the Mediterranean region only by Rome, was Alexandria, Egypt, the city founded by Alexander the Great. Although Rome now ruled Egypt, Alexandria continued to be a highly cosmopolitan city, and its library probably excelled anything in Rome as a center of intellectual activity. Basically the library was a university research center for all branches of the sciences, literary studies, and historical texts. One of its most distinguished associates in the middle of the second century was Claudius Ptolomaeus, famed for his work in astronomy, mathematics, optics, and geography.

Virtually nothing is known about this man, who has come down in history as Ptolemy. His name suggests he was Greek—he wrote his works in Greek—and he may have been related to the Ptolemies who had ruled Egypt for almost 300 years until the last of the dynasty, Cleopatra, died in 30 B.C. Ptolemy must have been born about the year A.D. 1 for he is known to have started his astronomical observations about the year A.D. 21. He published a series of groundbreaking works in the sciences, but almost all the original texts were lost and are known only because Arabic

Between about 200 B.C. and A.D. 500, Buddhist monks carved some 30 temples and monasteries into the interior of a rocky hillside at Ajanta in western India. Inside the temples were painted frescoes and elaborate sculptures. During much of this time, India was in turmoil, and about A.D. 500 Huns and other Central Asians moved down into northern India. (© *Philip Baird www.anthroarcheart.org*)

scholars translated them; these were eventually translated into Latin and later into other European languages.

The work that had the greatest influence on the Western world was his *Geography* and the maps that accompanied this. The original Greek text was the only work of its kind from the classical world that survived. The text provides a good sense of how Ptolemy viewed the earth, and his maps incorporated all that people outside Asia knew of the earth. He used a system of lines indicating latitudes and longitudes much like those in use today, and he even knew enough to curve them to account for the spherical shape of the Earth. Unfortunately, these lines become increasingly less accurate as he moved farther and farther beyond the Mediterranean area.

Ptolemy's understanding of the world was surprisingly accurate in some instances. He seemed to have quite detailed knowledge of the coastline of Britain (although he had Scotland turned on its side!). He recognized that the Caspian was a landlocked sea, not joined to the ocean as so many before him believed. He knew about the Carpathian

Mountains in eastern Europe, the Volga River in Russia, the sources of the Nile in two African lakes, the overland trade route from the Euphrates River to northern China. At the same time, there were many major errors. He did assume that there was some unknown *Terra Australis*—"southern land"—but he had it connecting the southern end of Africa to the southern corner of China (thus turning the Indian Ocean into a lake). Much of Germany, eastern Europe, and Russia were left blank; Scandinavia was an island; Sri Lanka was 14 times larger than it is; Africa was bisected by an east-west chain he called "Mountains of the Moon." Then he extended the Eurasian landmass eastward almost 40 percent farther than it is. And, most seriously of all, he misjudged the total circumference of the earth, making it almost 30 percent smaller than it is. Needless to say, he had no place on his maps reserved for the Americas.

Yet despite all these errors, Ptolemy's writings on geography and his maps were the most accurate to come out of the ancient world, and such was his reputation that they would remain the standard for centuries. This is not to say that the mass of people on earth—even in the non-Asian world—were even aware of Ptolemy's work. His writings vanished into obscure libraries, and his maps disappeared altogether. It was not until the 1400s, in fact, that European scholars began to

The Original Tourist
PAUSANIAS

Many Romans were widely traveled and many wrote down vast amounts of information about the known world. But it was left to a Greek from one of the empire's distant provinces to display a particular type of curiosity that has come to be associated in the modern world with tourists and their guidebooks. This was Pausanias, a Greek of whom little is known except that he probably came from Asia Minor (a region now part of modern Turkey) and flourished about A.D. 150. Judging from various remarks in his only known book, he may have been a doctor; he was also interested in bird watching. It is clear that he traveled at least through Palestine, Egypt, and parts of Italy, but above all, he visited all the major sites in central and southern Greece before he started setting down his observation about A.D. 155 in his *Itinerary of Greece* (often translated as *A Description* [or *Guide*] *to Greece*). Although written in Greek, this was the language known by most people who would have been in a position to travel in Greece—much as English has become the international travel language of today. It was filled with detailed descriptions and historical background about all the important classical sites but also with practical information about the road conditions and hints about how to save time or see lesser-known curiosities. The reason it stands out from other works of its time is that it is based not on others' books but on Pausanias's actual visits to every one of the places he describes. To this day, people can still visit these sites in Greece and use Pausanias's work as a guidebook.

As an indication of Ptolemy's reputation, the title page of Galileo's major work (1632) depicts Ptolemy between the most-revered ancient Greek philosopher, Aristotle, and Copernicus, the 16th-century astronomer who had established that the earth revolved around the sun. Galileo's book was composed as a dialogue between supporters of the Ptolemaic and Copernican systems. *(Library of Congress, Prints and Photographs Division [LC-USZ62-95172])*

Atlantic Islands

Among the more problematic examples of assigning priority to discoveries are the four island groups that lie off Europe and Africa out in the Atlantic Ocean: the Canaries, the Madeiras, the Azores, and the Cape Verde Islands. There is some support for the belief that the ancient Greeks may have heard rumors of the existence of the Madeira or Canary islands, for they located their version of Heaven in the Islands of the Blessed, or Fortunate Islands, off there in the Atlantic. That may be dismissed as mythology, but these four island groups did play major roles in the history of exploration, both in the ancient world and in later history.

The Canaries make up 13 islands; the closest of which is only 68 miles off the coast of northwestern Africa. The discovery of these islands is assigned to a king of Morocco, Juba, who flourished about 25 B.C. to A.D. 25. Juba, a North African Berber, wrote a book on the geography of North Africa (known only from Pliny the Elder) that reported he sponsored an expedition that came back with quite detailed and accurate information about the Canaries. (Ptolemy used these islands as the prime meridian—the starting point for his longitude lines of his map.) Juba's expedition identified six of the seven habitable islands and even reported signs of previous human habitation—including dogs and goats. At some time after this visit, people known as the Guanches came over from North Africa, but they were wiped out when the Spanish moved in early in the 1400s.

reconstruct his maps on the basis of his very detailed texts. By that time, scholarship in Europe had fallen into such a low state that Ptolemy was regarded as an absolute authority—something, by the way, he never claimed to be. His maps and texts would influence almost all the early explorers, including Columbus, and contribute to their miscalculations about the distances to be traveled and the location of lands.

THE DECLINE OF EXPLORATION

One of the reasons Ptolemy stood out so from the second century on was that, during the next 1,200 years, there were so few others who were doing anything comparable in the way of mapping the earth. At least in the West. From the third century, China was developing its own quite scientific system of mapmaking. But the Chinese shared the same limitation of Ptolemy's work: Their "scientific" maps were based on their astronomical observations and mathematical calculations, not on firsthand knowledge of the world, nor on the reports of mariners or travelers. In other words, they were not based on the information of explorers.

This was not necessarily the fault of the scholars. Not only were there very few libraries, there were no newspapers or periodicals in which to report current findings. For that matter, only a small elite was literate. There was a fundamental "disconnect" in all societies in that era—a lack of connection

The Madeiras are a group of two major and several smaller islands lying about 350 miles west of Morocco. It is possible that Carthaginian sailors discovered the main island of Madeira as early as 500 B.C. The next reference to human presence is in Plutarch, the Greek historian of the first century A.D.; he told about some sailors who in 80 B.C. sailed to "Atlantic Islands" that sound like the Madeiras. Nothing came of this, however, and the first known settlers were the Portuguese who came after the rediscovery of the islands by Portuguese in 1418–20.

The Azores comprise nine main islands located some 835 miles west of Portugal. There is a possibility, as mentioned previously, that Himilco, the Carthaginian who sailed out into the Atlantic about 500 B.C., may have come across the Azores. There has long been the claim that some ancient Phoenician coins were found on Cuervo Island in 1749, but most scholars do not take this as solid evidence. In fact, the first sign of their being known to Europeans was on a 14th century map, and Portuguese sailors only started visiting the Azores in 1427.

Finally, the Cape Verde islands include 10 main islands located about 350 miles west of Senegal, Africa. There is no evidence that they were known to the ancients; in fact, they do not seem to have been discovered until the Portuguese arrived there in 1460 and found them uninhabited.

between the theoretical and the actual, between the intellectual and the practical. Again this cannot be blamed entirely on the intellectuals, the literate elite; there was simply a lack of scientific knowledge, of technology, of inventions. They lacked the means to know exactly where rivers and mountains and lakes were located, to calculate precisely the distances between places on land as well as sea.

Rome, for instance, certainly counted many highly intelligent individuals within its far-flung boundaries. But few of them seem to have been interested in breaking new ground. Instead, they were more devoted to what might be called "secondhand scholarship." Some of the writers on geography and exploration during the early centuries of Roman

power have already been quoted—Posidonius (second century B.C.–first century B.C.), Strabo (first century B.C.–first century A.D.), Pomponius Mela (first century A.D.), Pliny the Elder (first century A.D.), Arrian (2nd century A.D.), Avienus (fourth century A.D.). Much is owed to these men—in many instances, they provide the sole accounts of early explorers and some of them even traveled to distant points in the Roman Empire.

But there does seem to have been another level to this "disconnect": Even people in a position to do so did not seem to be motivated to send forth or go forth to seek out new lands. Or if they did, and if they did write up reports, no records survived them. There were a few exceptions, among them the several surviving periploi (plural of *periplus*), meaning "circumnavigations." A few of the earlier ones have been drawn on already: the Massalian captain claimed by Avienus to have left an account of a sixth century B.C. voyage along the coast of Spain and all the way to the British Isles and Ireland; the account of Hanno's voyage down the northwestern coast of Africa; Nearchus's voyage from the Indus River to the Euphrates River; the account of Pytheas's voyage to Britain and the North Atlantic; the so-called *Periplus of Scylax*, describing the coasts of the Mediterranean and Black Seas; the second century B.C. Agatharchides' description of the coasts of the Red Sea; the first century A.D., *Periplus of the Erythraean Sea*, describing the route from Egypt to India and along the east coast of Africa.

There were several more of these in the later part of the Roman Empire. In A.D. 131, Arrian, the Roman historian who preserved the story of the epic voyage of Nearchus, Alexander's admiral, also wrote a *Periplus of the Euxine Sea*, a guide to the coast of the Black Sea. *The Stadiasmus of the Great Sea*, dated to sometime in the third or fourth centuries, was a guide to a large section of the coast of the Mediterranean Sea; it not only gave fairly exact distances but provided information about harbors and depths of water along the way. Another such work of this era, dated about A.D. 400 and attributed to a Marcianus of Heraclea, a Greek city, was a guide to the "Outer Seas," which referred to the Indian and Atlantic oceans.

The land-based equivalent of these periploi were "road-books." *The Parthian Stations* of Isadore of Charax has been mentioned as recording the route from Mesopotamia to India during the reign of Augustus. The *Itinerarium Antonini* of about A.D. 200 records the main routes and towns throughout the Roman Empire at that time. The *Jerusalem Itinerary* dated to the fourth century A.D., provides detailed instructions for Christian pilgrims to make their way from France across Italy to Constantinople and then down as far as Antioch, then a center of Christianity in Syria.

SHUTTING DOWN

As remarkable and informative as the many periploi and road-books were, these were all guides to known places. They all "wrapped up" the world rather than left it open-ended. What is notable, too, is that almost none of the historians or compilers of guides were themselves Romans, nor did the stories the historians preserve or recount about explorers involve Romans. The Chinese of this era were the opposite in the sense that they wrote about and charted only Chinese expeditions, but they were like the Romans in that they were not interested in striking out into the unknown. In fact, for all their careful work in the fields of geography and mapmaking, the Chinese did not show much interest in exploring the world far beyond their borders. Perhaps the symbol of this was the Great Wall: True, it was designed to hold off potentially hostile neighbors, but by A.D. 500 it had come to symbolize China's determination to remain isolated.

It was almost as though the world needed to take a break about the year 500. By this time, all the world's major landmasses were inhabited—the exception, of course, being Antarctica, which would not be inhabited until the 20th century. The world's population around the year A.D. 500 has been estimated to have been about 300 million to 500 million at most. This was not that many by today's standard, but plenty of people to go around. Mountain ranges and deserts remained off-limits—again, as most are to this day—and many large expanses of land were still uninhabited. Many isolated islands far off in the oceans were still unknown and uninhabited; the most outstanding instance was New Zealand, for it would probably not be until sometime between A.D. 750 and 1000 that the first humans came ashore there—Maoris from Polynesian islands to the north of New Zealand. Some ancestors of modern Inuit had made their way to Greenland centuries before A.D. 500, but there is some question as to whether they were permanent inhabitants at that time; in any case, it was still unknown to Europeans. Iceland may have been known to European sailors but was still uninhabited by anyone. But Madagascar, the last of the world's largest islands to remain unsettled, now had people who had come over from

Construction of the Great Wall of China had begun about 220 B.C. during the Qin dynasty and continued for another 1,700 years. Designed to hold off tribes from the north, it never fully succeeded in doing so, but it did come to symbolize China's desire to isolate itself. *(Library of Congress, Prints and Photographs Division [LC-USZ62-70830])*

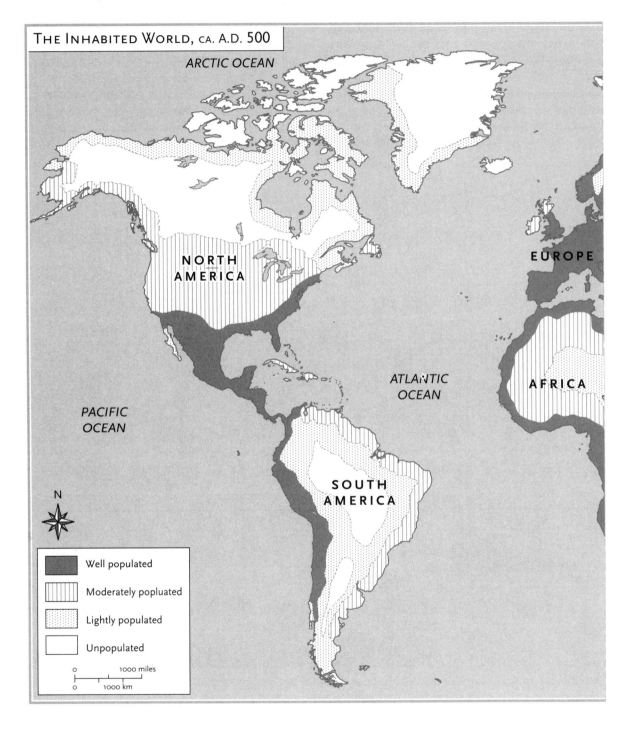

THE INHABITED WORLD, CA. A.D. 500

ARCTIC OCEAN

NORTH AMERICA

EUROPE

PACIFIC OCEAN

ATLANTIC OCEAN

AFRICA

SOUTH AMERICA

N

Well populated

Moderately popluated

Lightly populated

Unpopulated

0   1000 miles

0   1000 km

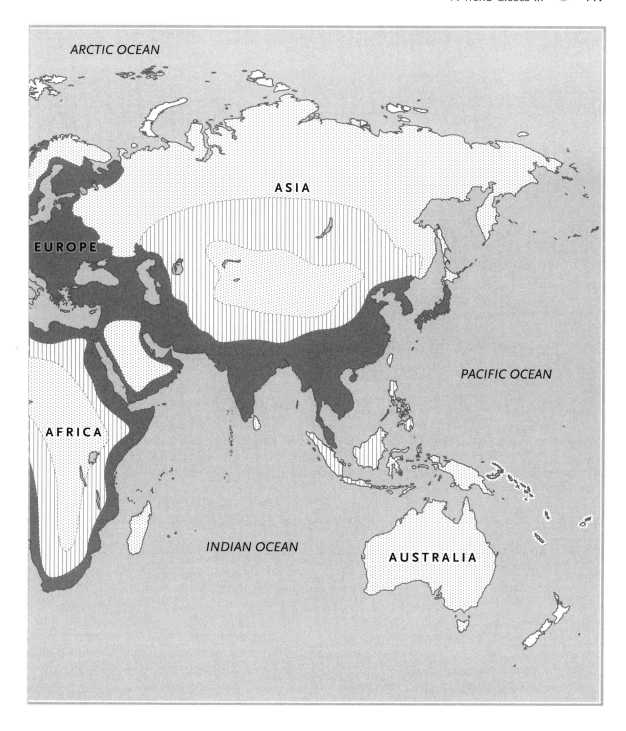

ARCTIC OCEAN

ASIA

EUROPE

PACIFIC OCEAN

AFRICA

INDIAN OCEAN

AUSTRALIA

By A.D. 500, human beings were living in some of most remote and inhospitable regions of the world, including the Alaskan coast inhabited by the ancestors of the modern Aleut people. This drawing of the late 1700s, which accompanied Captain James Cook's account of his voyage to the region, depicts the people of Oonalashka on the Alaskan peninsula in their canoes. *(Library of Congress, Prints and Photographs Division [LC-USZ62-102244])*

Indonesia, and Africa. Virtually every corner of Africa, Asia, and Europe were known to and settled by at least some people, even if they were only nomadic tribes. And although it was unknown to the rest of the world, the entire Western Hemisphere, from the Arctic region to the tip of South America, was at least sparsely inhabited.

By the year 500, much of the world did seem to be in disarray, if not in complete turmoil. The Roman Empire had split into Western and Eastern empires in 395, and by 476, after decades of being battered by various tribesmen, the last Western emperor was removed by a Germanic leader, Odoacer. War between the tribes of Europe and the Eastern empire soon followed. China, too, was divided into northern and southern kingdoms, which in turn were under attack from both internal and foreign forces. India, which had flourished under the Gupta Empire since A.D. 320, was likewise being torn apart by both invaders from Central Asia and competing Indian kingdoms. It was not a time conducive to setting out for new lands. New generations and new peoples would have to take up the search.

But ancient peoples were handing over an impressive legacy. Their view of the world was greatly flawed—full of gaps, misconceptions, errors; even the best-informed people still had no conception of the true locations and dimensions of most of the earth's territories beyond their immediate regions. Ancient peoples' motives for moving into new territories, moreover, were often less than noble, their methods even brutal. Yet people today should hesitate before finding fault with these ancients. Just consider what they endured to travel to distant points! The

The Great Serpent Mound is located in south-central Ohio and, although scholars differ as to exactly which group of Native Americans built it, it almost certainly existed by A.D. 500. Some 1,340 feet long and about three feet high on average, it represents both the advanced technological skills and mythological/religious thinking of North Americans of this time. *(Library of Congress)*

By A.D. 500, the Maya were flourishing across Central America, and one of their chief centers was Copán (in present-day Honduras). Ball courts like this in Copán were found at many Maya (and Aztec) sites, and the game—which involved knocking a small rubber ball through a vertical hoop—clearly had some religious significance. In some instances, in fact, it appears that the losers were decapitated as sacrifices. *(© Philip Baird www.anthroarcheart.org)*

discomforts and dangers of sea voyages and overland treks can hardly be imagined by people accustomed to modern travel. The ancient world definitely deserves recognition for contributing its share to the history of discoveries and explorations.

WHAT CHARACTERIZES ANCIENT EXPLORERS?

If many ancient peoples—both individuals and societies—deserve great credit for their contributions to the discovery and exploration of new lands, it is also true that many others did not engage in this activity. Just why have some peoples shown no interest in seeking out new lands? This is a question that arises not only in the ancient world but that also hovers across all of history.

Even several of the ancient peoples encountered in this book have shown lesser interest than others in exploring new lands. The Egyptians, for example, were largely content to stay close to the Nile and trade with nearby neighbors. The Romans, for all their far-flung conquests, for all the vast territory they dominated, did not seem to take much initiative in seeking out the unknown. The Chinese are yet a different case: For many centuries they did send out expeditions—and then they stopped this and drew within their circle.

Meanwhile, there are those ancient peoples who seem to have shown no interest in moving outside their own culture's base—people such as the Maya of Central America. The Maya began to emerge as a distinctive culture as early as 1500 B.C., attaining the height of their civilization between about A.D. 200–800. During this long period of time they made astronomical observations that allowed them to work out extremely precise calendars; they developed a system of numbering that was sophisticated enough to include something like a zero; they developed a system of writing more advanced than any used by contemporaneous Native Americans; they developed technically sound architecture and built ambitious ceremonial centers; they constructed stone-surfaced roads and irrigation

About A.D. 500, northern India was invaded by an aggressive people from Central Asia known as the Huna in Indian history and as Huns in European history. The Huns had invaded the Roman Empire in the 300s and 400s before finally being expelled. Although they were also expelled from India by about 550, they opened the way for other Central Asian peoples to invade northern India. *(Library of Congress, Prints and Photographs Division [LC-USZ62-72759])*

systems; they traded a variety of products over great distances, primarily with their fellow Maya, often using large canoes that moved along the coast.

Yet for all these accomplishments, the Maya do not seem to have ever ventured very far from their own homeland, a relatively confined region extending from Mexico's Yucatán Peninsula in the west to the highlands of Guatemala in the east. Even their wars—and there were many—were conducted among themselves: They seemed to show no interest in expansion. By the same token, they showed no interest in exploration. They are one of the prime examples of a self-contained society.

A totally different type of society was embodied by the Huns. They were a nomadic Mongol people originally based in the steppes of Mongolia. Some scholars believe that they were the people known to the Chinese as the Xiongnu (Hsiung-nu) who began to invade northern China as early as the second century B.C. In any case, by the fourth century A.D. the people known to Europeans as the Huns were based in Central Asia, over near the Caspian Sea. As early as 350 they crossed the Volga River and moved into what it now Hungary. Led by Attila between 433 and 450, Huns moved westward into Europe, and eventually Attila ruled an empire extending from the Caspian Sea in the east to the Rhine River in the west. Not satisfied with this, Attila invaded Gaul (modern France) and northern Italy, but a combination of local peoples, Roman troops, famine, and disease stopped the Huns. After Attila was killed in a battle north of present-day Venice in 1453, the Huns retreated to Asia. It is possible that some of these retreating Huns were the same people known as the Huna who invaded northern India starting about A.D. 500. Driven out of India by about 550, the Huna, as well as the Huns, pretty much vanish from history.

The Huns, then, were the complete opposite of the Maya. They were almost always on the move over a vast territory, establishing no major cities, developing no important culture, and leaving no material remains. Instead of being self-contained, they exist almost entirely as a people who intruded on other peoples. Yet like the Maya, they seem to have shown no interest in sending out individuals to find or explore new lands: The Huns were interested only in taking over land inhabited by others.

Whether the Maya and the Huns represent the only two types of ancient societies—settled/self-contained and nomadic/expansive—that showed no interest in discovering and exploring new lands is not the point here. Certainly many other instances might be cited to establish that not all ancient peoples were interested in the discovery and exploration of new lands. Just why this is so, just what distinguishes explorer cultures from nonexplorer cultures, whether there are some underlying and unifying factors—these are all questions that might lead to stimulating discussions.

Attempts to find some single factor to "explain" the success or lack of success of previous societies have always ended up being discarded. This would certainly be the case if there were a claim about some single factor that "makes" a society engage in exploration. But one thing is clear: The ancient people —again, both individuals and societies—described in this volume's chapters do seem to have shared at least one characteristic: The ability to consider the unknown, to recognize that something must lie beyond familiar borders.

GLOSSARY

astrolabe   An instrument invented as early as 200 B.C. to measure the level of elevation, or altitude, of the sun, stars, or planets. Originally used by astronomers (*astrolabe* in Greek means "star taker"), it would eventually be adapted for use in navigation.

cauldron   A large vessel usually used for boiling liquids.

circumnavigate   The term is from the Latin for "sailing around," and refers to sailing around a large body of land, whether an island, a continent, or the entire earth.

cuneiform   The system of writing employing small wedge-shaped (Latin *cuneus* means "wedge") elements pressed into wet clay tablets by a stylus (see **stylus**). It was invented by the ancient Sumerians about 2500 B.C. and adopted by many of the peoples who lived across Mesopotamia and Persia during the next 2,500 years.

dead reckoning   A method long used by navigators to estimate the position of a ship at sea based on such factors as the time in passage from a known point, the (estimated) speed of the ship, and changes of direction in relation to (noninstrument aided) observations of celestial bodies. The term *dead* is thought to come from the word *deduce*, meaning to trace from a beginning.

Druid   A member of an order of priests in the religion practiced in ancient Gaul and Britain. The word has come to be applied to anyone who practices that religion.

dynasty   A succession of rulers from the same family or line that maintains a certain continuity of practices.

estuary   The point at which a river's mouth meets the sea and so the ocean's tides affect the river's current.

fossil   The remains—usually only a part but they could be complete—of a plant or animal that had lived in the distant past. (*Skeleton* is usually used to refer to bones less than many thousands of years old.) The term may also refer to traces of living organisms, such as footprints or outlines of a plant. Often it refers to bones of human or other animals that have been embedded and preserved in earth or rock.

gnomon   A device that casts a shadow from the sun and is used as an indicator of time or location; a sundial is the most familiar example.

head   When used in connection with a body of water, it refers to the top, or closed end, of a gulf or bay.

hominid   A member of the family that includes the direct ancestors of human beings as well as all living human beings. It is generally recognized that the hominid line began about 5 million years ago.

Homo erectus Latin for "upright man," this term refers to the stage in human evolution extending from about 1,750,000 to 750,000 years ago, the time when the ancestors of modern humans first began to walk in an erect position.

Homo sapiens Latin for "knowledgeable" or "wise" man, this term refers to the species of human being that first appeared about 160,000 years ago and to which all modern humans belong.

homogeneous All of the same or similar kind.

insurrection An open revolt or uprising against a civil authority or established government; often it is begun by a small and relatively unorganized group, and it may at least start with civil disobedience rather than warfare.

interstices In the context of mining, it refers to narrow spaces in rocks where the desired mineral is located.

Inuit The major group of Arctic people living across northern Canada and Greenland. This name is now preferred instead of Eskimo, which among other problems fails to distinguish among various other Arctic peoples such as the Aleut and Yup'ik.

jade One of two minerals—jadeite or nephrite—that are usually pale green or white stones. When polished, jade is used either as gemstones or for carvings.

kybernetes A Greek word for "governor" or "controller," it was the ancient Greeks' term for a ship's helmsman. In the 20th century, it was adopted for *cybernetics,* the study of control processes in biological, mechanical, and electronic systems, and from this the word *cyber* was spun off to be applied to many things related to computers.

lacquerware Objects whose surface has been treated with lacquer, originally a natural resin from the lacquer tree found only in Asia. In modern times, a lacquer finish may be applied with synthetic compounds. Lacquerware has a hard, shiny surface.

latitude The angular distance north or south of the earth's equator and measured in degrees. Sometimes referred to as a *parallel,* there are 90 degrees between the equator and each of the poles.

li A standard ancient Chinese unit of measurement of distances; although there is some disagreement as to its exact equivalent, most scholars consider it to equal about 1/3 a mile.

longitude The angular distance east or west of the modern prime meridian, Greenwich, England. It is measured in degrees; there are 360 degrees altogether, measured as up to 180 degrees east or west of Greenwich.

middleman In commercial transactions, an individual who buys from producers or other traders and then sells to other traders, merchants, or consumers.

monsoon A major wind system that reverses directions seasonally and thereby affects large climatic areas. In southern Asia in particular, it is a wind from the south or southwest that brings heavy rains in the summer, and the first mariners from Europe had to learn about the monsoon in order to plan their voyages in the region.

nomadic Describing a group of people who have no permanent home but move—usually according to the seasons—in search of food and water for themselves or grazing lands for their animals.

pathogen Any biological agent that causes disease; it usually refers to living microorganisms such as bacteria or fungi or to viruses.

periplus (plural *periploi*) From the Greek word for "sailing around," this term is used for the published directions for mariners for coastal routes and points of interest along these routes.

pilgrimage A trip undertaken to a sacred place or religious shrine.

praetor A Roman official, originally a supervisor of the administration of justice. Over time, the position changed, becoming more like a military magistrate in the provinces. Under the empire, the praetors returned to being administrators of the law, but their power declined and the title became little more than honorary.

quern A stone, usually with a recessed surface, on which grain or other crops are ground by a hand-held tool.

rationalist An individual who believes in relying on reason as the best guide to understanding and activity. In ancient Greek history, this was applied to the school of intellectuals who first appeared in Ionia, the Greek-based region along the coast of Turkey, and it characterized many Greek philosophers' approach to life.

reed The stalk of various tall perennial grasses, hollow stemmed and usually fairly tough, that can be used to make anything from a shelter to a boat.

stylus The instrument used to write cuneiform, its sharp end is wedge-shaped—that is, slightly wider at one tip than the opposite.

truss A rigid framework designed to support a structure; in the case of shipbuilding, it would be a horizontal beam extending between the two sides of a hull to maintain the ship's shape.

wattle A structure made of poles intertwined with branches, twigs, or reeds; the term may also refer simply to the materials used to make such a structure.

FURTHER INFORMATION

NONFICTION

Aubet, Maria Eugenia. *The Phoenicians and the West: Politics, Colonies and Trade.* Cambridge, England: Cambridge University Press, 2001.

Barton, Miles. *Prehistoric America: A Journey through the Ice Age and Beyond.* New Haven: Yale University Press, 2003.

Bosworth, A. B. *Conquest and Empire: The Reign of Alexander the Great.* Cambridge, England: Cambridge University Press. 1993.

Bunson, Matthew. *Encyclopedia of the Roman Empire.* Rev. ed. New York: Facts On File, 2002.

Burton, Harry E. *The Discovery of the Ancient World.* Cambridge: Harvard University Press, 1932.

Caesar, Julius. *The Conquest of Gaul.* Trans. by S. A. Hanford. New York: Viking Press, 1983.

Cary, M. and E. H. Warmington. *The Ancient Explorers.* London: Methuen & Co., 1929.

Casson, Lionel. *The Ancient Mariners: Seafarers and Sea Fighters of the Mediterranean in Ancient Times.* New York: Macmillan, 1959.

———. *Ships and Seamanship in the Ancient World.* Princeton, New Jersey: Princeton University Press, 1971.

Cavalli-Sforza, Luigi Luca. *The Great Human Diaspora: The History of Diversity and Evolution.* Trans. by Sarah Thorne. Cambridge, Mass.: Perseus Publishing, 1996.

Cunliffe, Barry. *The Extraordinary Voyage of Pytheas the Greek.* Rev. ed. New York: Walker & Co., 2003.

De Solla Price, Derek. "An Ancient Greek Computer." *Scientific American.* Vol. 200, No. 6, June 1959, pp. 60–67.

Dillehay, Thomas. *The Settlement of the Americas.* New York: Basic Books, 2000.

Fagan, Brian. *People of the Earth: An Introduction to World Prehistory.* (With CD) Upper Saddle River, NJ: Prentice Hall, 2000.

Fraington, Karen, ed. *Historical Atlas of Expeditions.* New York: Facts On File, 2001.

Fox, Robin Lane. *Alexander the Great.* New York: Penguin Group (USA), 1994.

Gaines, Ann Graham. *Herodotus and the Explorers of the Classical Age.* New York: Chelsea House, 1993.

Fraser, P. M. *Ptolemaic Alexandria.* Oxford: Clarendon Press, 1972.

Herodotus. *The Histories.* Trans. by Aubrey de Selincourt. New York: Penguin Group (USA), 2003.

Higham, Charles F. W. *Encyclopedia of Ancient Asian Civilizations.* New York: Facts On File, 2004.

Hopkirk, Peter. *Foreign Devils on the Silk Road: The Search for the Lost Cities and Treasures of Chinese Central Asia.* Amherst, Mass.: University of Massachusetts Press, 1984.

Lambert, David, ed. *Encyclopedia of Prehistory.* New York: Facts On File, 2002.

Lauber, Patricia. *Who Came First? New Clues to Prehistoric America.* Washington, D.C.: National Geographic, 2003.

Markoe, Glenn. *Phoenicians.* Berkeley: University of California Press, 2001.

Morkot, Robert, ed. *The Penguin Atlas of Ancient Greece.* New York: Penguin Group (USA), 1997.

Needham, Joseph. *Science and Civilization in China.* Volume 3, Section 22. Cambridge, England: The University Press, 1959.

Obregon, Maurice. *Beyond the Edge of the Sea: Sailing with Jason and the Argonauts, Ulysses, the Vikings and Other Explorers of the Ancient World.* New York: Modern Library, 2002.

Pary, J. H. *The Discovery of the Sea.* Berkeley: University of California Press, 1981.

Pausanias. *Guide to Greece.* Trans. by Peter Levi. 2 Vols. Baltimore: New York: Penguin Group (USA), 1971.

Roseman, Christina Horst. *Pytheas of Massalia: On the Ocean: Text, Translation and Commentary.* Chicago: Ares Publishing, 1994.

Scarre, Chris, ed. *Penguin Historical Atlas of Ancient Rome.* New York: Penguin Group (USA), 1995.

Shoff, Wilfred H. *The Periplus of the Erythraean Sea: Travel and Trade in the Indian Ocean by a Merchant of the First Century.* New York: Longmans Green, 1912.

———. *The Periplus of Hanno: A Voyage of Discovery Down the West Coast of Africa.* Philadelphia: Commercial Museum, 1912.

Sorenson, John L., and Martin Raish. *Pre-Columbian Contact with the Americas Across the Ocean: An Annotated Bibliography.* 2nd ed. rev. Provo, Utah: Research Press, 1996.

Spekke, Arnolds. *The Ancient Amber Routes and the Geographic Discovery of the Eastern Baltic.* Chicago: Ares Publishing, 1976.

Stockwell, Foster, and Sharon L. Lechter. *Westerners in China: A History of Exploration and Trade, Ancient Times Through the Present.* Jefferson, NC: McFarland & Co., 2002.

Strabo. *The Geography.* Trans. by H. L. Jones. 8 vols. Cambridge: Harvard University Press, 1960–67.

Thomson, J. Oliver. *History of Ancient Geography.* Cambridge, England: The University Press, 1948.

Tozer, Henry F. *A History of Ancient Geography.* 2nd ed. rev. Cambridge, England: Cambridge University Press, 1935.

Van Sertima, Ivan. *They Came Before Columbus.* New York: Random House, 1976.

Warmington, E. H. *The Commerce between the Roman Empire and India.* London: Octagon Books, 2nd rev. ed., 1974.

Wachsmann, Shelley. *Seagoing Ships and Seamanship in the Bronze Age Levant.* College Station: Texas A&M University Press, 1998.

Wauchope, Robert. *Lost Tribes & Sunken Continents.* Illinois: University of Chicago Press, 1962.

FICTION

Bell, Albert A., Jr. *All Roads Lead to Murder.* Stratford, Victoria, Australia: Publishing, Ltd., 2002.

Cole, Les. *The Sea Kings.* Ventura, Calif.: House of Adda Press, 1996.

Ford, Michael Curtis. *The Ten Thousand.* New York: St. Martin's Press, 2002.

Leckie, Ross. *Carthage.* Edinburgh, Scotland: Canongate Books, 2001.

Manfredi, Valerio. *Alexander—The Ends of the Earth.* New York: Washington Square Press, 2002.

Renault, Mary. *Fire from Heaven.* New York: Vintage Books, 2002.

———. *Funeral Games.* New York: Vintage Books, 2002.

———. *The Persian Boy.* New York: Vintage Books, 1998.

Scarrow, Simon. *Under the Eagle: A Tale of Military Adventures and Reckless Heroes with the Roman Legions.* New York: St. Martin's Press, 2001.

Turteltaub, H. N. *Over the Wine Dark Sea.* New York: Tor Books, 2002.

Vidal, Gore. *Creation.* New York: Doubleday, 2002.

Waltari, Mika. *The Egyptian.* Illinois: Chicago Review Press, 2003.

VHS/DVD

Ancient China (1998). Schlessinger Media, VHS, 1998.

Ancient Egyptians (2003). Granada International, VHS/DVD, 2003.

Carthage and the Phoenicians (2000). Choices, Inc., VHS, 2000.

Cleopatra's World: Alexandria Revealed (2001). A&E Home Video, VHS, 2001.

Dawn of Man—The Story of Human Evolution (2001). BBC, VHS, 2002.

Egypt's Golden Empire (2002). Warner Home Video, VHS/DVD, 2003.

The Greeks: Crucible of Civilization (1999). PBS Home Video, VHS/DVD, 2000.

Hail Caesar (2000). A&E Entertainment, VHS, 2000.

In the Footsteps of Alexander the Great (2000). PBS Home Video, VHS, 2001.

Lost Civilizations: Egypt, Mesopotamia, Egypt (1994). Time-Life Videos, VHS, 1995.

Lost Ships of the Mediterranean (2000). National Geographic, VHS, 2001.

Mystery of the First American (2000). Nova/WGBH, VHS, 2000.

BIB:*The Roman Empire in the First Century* (2000). PBS Home Video, VHS, 2001.

Roman Roads—Paths to Empire (1999). A&E Home Video. VHS, 2000.

Rome: Power and Glory (1998). Questar Inc., DVD, 1999.

Silk Road (1991). Central Park Media, VHS, Vol. I, 1991. Vol. II, 1998. DVD, 2000.

The Silk Road of the Sea (1991). PBS, VHS, 1991.

WEB SITES

Early Humans

HOMO SAPIENS EVOLUTION

Smithsonian Institution, National Museum of Natural History, Human Origins Program. Available online. URL: http://www.mnh.si.edu/anthro/humanorigins/. Downloaded on June 19, 2003.

HOMO SAPIENS DISPERSAL

Early Modern *Homo sapiens*. Available online. URL: http://www.anthro.palomar.edu/homo2/modern_humans.htm. Updated on May 5, 2003.

Early Explorers

PYTHEAS OF MASSALIA

American Hellenic Educational Progressive Association, Fifth District, Articles. Available online. URL: http://www.ahepafamily.org/d5/pytheas.html. Downloaded on June 19, 2003.

EXPLORERS FROM PRE-GREEK LANDS

The First Explorers. Available online. URL: http://www.win.tue.nl/~engles/discovery/ancient.html. Downloaded on June 19, 2003.

PHOENICIANS

A Bequest Unearthed, Phoenicia. Available online. URL: http://phoenicia.org. Downloaded on June 19, 2003.

Greece

EXPLORERS FROM GREECE

Greek Explorers. Available online. URL: http://www.win.tue.nl/~engles/discovery/greece.html. Downloaded on June 19, 2003.

GREEK SHIPS AND SEAFARING

Ships of the Ancient Greeks on the World-Wide Web. Available online. URL: http://www.bulfinch.org/fables/grkship.html. Downloaded on June 19, 2003.

Rome

ROMAN EMPIRE HISTORY

Illustrated History of the Roman Empire. Available online. URL: http://roman-empire.net. Downloaded on June 19, 2003.

Asia

SILK ROAD

Silk Road. Available online. URL: http://www.ess.uci.edu/~oliver/silk.html. Downloaded on June 19, 2003.

CHINESE HISTORY

China the Beautiful: Chinese History. Available online. URL: http://www.chinapage.com/history1.html. Downloaded on June 19, 2003.

History Link 101, Ancient China. Available online. URL: http://www.historylink101.com/china_history.htm. Downloaded on June 19, 2003.

INDEX

Page numbers in *italics* indicate a photograph. Page numbers followed by *m* indicate maps. Page numbers followed by *g* indicate glossary entries. Page numbers in **boldface** indicate box features.